T0270619

Overcoming Barriers to Working with Highly Capable Allies and Partners in the Air, Space, and Cyber Domains

An Exploratory Analysis

JENNIFER D. P. MORONEY, STEPHANIE PEZARD, DAVID E. THALER,
GENE GERMANOVICH, BETH GRILL, BRUCE MCCLINTOCK,
KAREN SCHWINDT, MARY KATE ADGIE, ANIKA BINNENDIJK,
KEVIN J. CONNOLLY, KATIE FEISTEL, JEFFREY W. HORNUNG,
ALISON K. HOTTES, MOON KIM, ISABELLE NAZHA, GABRIELLE TARINI,
MARK TOUKAN, JALEN ZEMAN

Prepared for the Department of the Air Force
Approved for public release; distribution unlimited

PROJECT AIR FORCE

For more information on this publication, visit **www.rand.org/t/RRA968-1**.

About RAND

The RAND Corporation is a research organization that develops solutions to public policy challenges to help make communities throughout the world safer and more secure, healthier and more prosperous. RAND is nonprofit, nonpartisan, and committed to the public interest. To learn more about RAND, visit www.rand.org.

Research Integrity

Our mission to help improve policy and decisionmaking through research and analysis is enabled through our core values of quality and objectivity and our unwavering commitment to the highest level of integrity and ethical behavior. To help ensure our research and analysis are rigorous, objective, and nonpartisan, we subject our research publications to a robust and exacting quality-assurance process; avoid both the appearance and reality of financial and other conflicts of interest through staff training, project screening, and a policy of mandatory disclosure; and pursue transparency in our research engagements through our commitment to the open publication of our research findings and recommendations, disclosure of the source of funding of published research, and policies to ensure intellectual independence. For more information, visit www.rand.org/about/research-integrity.

RAND's publications do not necessarily reflect the opinions of its research clients and sponsors.

Library of Congress Cataloging-in-Publication Data is available for this publication.

ISBN: 978-1-9774-1155-6

Cover: Left: U.S. Navy photo by Chief Mass Communication Specialist Shannon E. Renfroe; middle: Drawing of the U.S. Military's Wideband Global SATCOM (WGS) satellites/U.S. Air Force Space Command photo illustration; right: Cyber connections and data around the world/Piranka/Getty Images.

About This Report

This research was undertaken within the RAND Corporation's Project AIR FORCE division and is part of a series of projects on security cooperation approaches and investments that help to inform Department of the Air Force investments. Through 11 case studies, this research focuses on the barriers that exist to collaborating with highly capable allies and partners and should be considered exploratory, given the limited research completed to date on this topic. The research was undertaken for the Deputy Under Secretary of the Air Force for International Affairs in collaboration with several other Department of the Air Force offices.

The research reported here was commissioned by the Deputy Under Secretary of the Air Force for International Affairs and conducted within the Strategy and Doctrine Program of RAND Project AIR FORCE as part of a fiscal year 2021 project, "Barriers to Competing More Effectively Across the Air, Space and Cyber Domains."

RAND Project AIR FORCE

RAND Project AIR FORCE (PAF), a division of the RAND Corporation, is the Department of the Air Force's (DAF's) federally funded research and development center for studies and analyses, supporting both the United States Air Force and the United States Space Force. PAF provides the DAF with independent analyses of policy alternatives affecting the development, employment, combat readiness, and support of current and future air, space, and cyber forces. Research is conducted in four programs: Strategy and Doctrine; Force Modernization and Employment; Resource Management; and Workforce, Development, and Health. The research reported here was prepared under contract FA7014-16-D-1000.

Additional information about PAF is available on our website: www.rand.org/paf/

This report documents work originally shared with the DAF on August 18, 2021. The draft report, issued in October 2021, was reviewed by formal peer reviewers and DAF subject-matter experts.

Acknowledgments

We wish to first and foremost thank our sponsor, the Secretary of the Air Force for International Affairs (SAF/IA) Strategy and Plans Division; Gordon Ettenson and his team; and, especially, Tiana Jackson for their support. We worked closely with several key colleagues in SAF/IA, as well as Headquarters Air Force A5-8 under LeeAnn Borman and her team, at Pacific Air Forces in A5I under Col Daniel Munter, and at U.S. Space Command and U.S. Cyber Command. The success of this research absolutely depended on allied and partner official input, and we are particularly grateful to those individuals we spoke to from Australia, the United

Kingdom, Norway, Japan, Estonia, Finland, and Italy for their time and insights. We also wish to thank Meagan McKernan and Maj Gen (Ret) Steve Oliver for their extremely helpful comments and inputs, as well as Clifford Grammich for his skillful editing of an earlier version of this draft.

Summary

Issue

The Department of the Air Force (DAF), like the entire U.S. Department of Defense (DoD), has been directed to support the National Defense Strategy objectives of defending the homeland and deterring strategic attacks against the United States and its allies and partners. The National Defense Strategy stresses that mutually beneficial alliances and partnerships are critical to achieving U.S. objectives and calls on DoD to incorporate ally and partner perspectives, competencies, and advantages at every stage of defense planning.[1] This report is the first of a two-volume set of reports in which we consider how the DAF and DoD can enhance engagement with highly capable allies and partners to improve interoperability by exploring the following key questions:

- What are some of the main barriers to security cooperation (SC) with highly capable allies and partners?
- What workarounds, if any, have been or could be created?

In this first volume, we create a typology of the barriers that impede SC with highly capable allies and partners; identify some of the more specific barriers in the air, space, and cyber domains; suggest mitigation strategies for each of these barriers; and propose a preliminary approach for implementing some of these mitigation strategies. In the second volume, we provide a similar overview, as well as the supporting analysis of 11 case studies.[2]

Approach

This work is the first of its kind and is meant to document barriers to working with allies and partners, as well as the benefits and risks. Although the case studies are few in number, they allowed us to begin to identify barrier mitigation strategies. The case studies document key barriers and allow for a deep conversation, from both the U.S. and the allied and partner perspective, regarding the issues that exist within the confines of each case study.

---

[1] DoD, "Fact Sheet: 2022 National Defense Strategy," March 28, 2022.

[2] Jennifer D. P. Moroney, Stephanie Pezard, David E. Thaler, Gene Germanovich, Beth Grill, Bruce McClintock, Karen Schwindt, Mary Kate Adgie, Anika Binnendijk, Kevin J. Connolly, Katie Feistel, Jeffrey W. Hornung, Alison K. Hottes, Moon Kim, Isabelle Nazha, Gabrielle Tarini, Mark Toukan, and Jalen Zeman, *Overcoming Barriers to Working with Highly Capable Allies and Partners in the Air, Space, and Cyber Domains: Case Studies*, Santa Monica, Calif.: RAND Corporation, RR-A968-2, 2023, Not available to the general public.

Major Features

We find that barriers fall into the categories outlined in the typology shown in Table S.1.

Table S.1. Barriers Typology

Type of Barrier	Representative examples
Budgetary	• Differences in funding priorities or availability of resources • Inability to determine or agree to fair share (costing requirements)
Bureaucratic	• Sheer number of stakeholders and organizations • Over-classification of communications (default to NOFORN) • Conflicting priorities and incentives within U.S. and partner organizations
Cultural	• Differing approaches or expectations regarding military cooperation • Reluctance or inability to share sensitive or classified data • Historical experience in bilateral or multilateral engagements/relationships
Political	• Governmental restrictions or limitations external to DoD or MoD • Domestic pressures or influences from industry, legislatures, or popular opinion
Regulatory	• Written prohibitions or limitations to collaboration in U.S. legal code, Congressional legislation, or departmental instructions • Ally/partner legal or executive-level restrictions on collaboration with foreign partners
Strategic	• Diverging national interests and threat perceptions • Differences in priorities re: collaboration with U.S. and other allies and partners
Technical	• Lack of compatible systems or procedures to share information • Imbalances in scientific or domain expertise • Lack of confidence in ally/partner's ability to protect effectively classified or sensitive information

NOTE: MoD = Ministry of Defense; NOFORN = Not Releasable to Foreign Nationals.

Major Findings

In these 11 case studies, we identified several barriers to cooperation with highly capable allies and partners; some are within individual domains, and many are across domains (meaning more than one domain but not necessarily across all three). Although some of these barriers might be well-known to many SC practitioners, we document them in relation to specific cases. Our case studies suggest the following key findings:

- One of our air case studies suggests that differences in strategic priorities (i.e., that the United States seeks to create new capabilities, while an ally or partner wishes to obtain U.S. technology) can lead to unrealized expectations and diminished cooperation.
- Our space case studies suggest that
  - the large size and complexity of space programs and the lack of a single voice across the U.S. space SC enterprise challenge the scale and pace of collaboration
  - the DAF and other U.S. organizations appear to have insufficient human resources to enable the level of space SC envisioned by strategy.
- Our cyber case studies suggest that

- the United States and its allies and partners often have differing views over what they consider to be "sensitive" information
- similar to the space community, the cyber community suffers from the lack of a single voice within the cybersecurity cooperation enterprise, which somewhat explains the lack of advocacy for, and clear prioritization of, the agreements that the United States should be pursuing and the types of technology it should be developing with allies and partners.

- Across domains, our case studies suggest that
  - allies and partners are rarely included in concept and system development phases
  - the extent and speed of communication between the United States and its allies and partners are limited
  - there are technical collaborative infrastructure constraints that inhibit the ability of the United States and its allies and partners to share information
  - slow bureaucratic execution can impede SC
  - some U.S. regulations impede rather than support SC, particularly with fast-evolving technologies
  - failure to account for a partner's political constraints can slow cooperation activities
  - there is an overall lack of incentive, tasking, and understanding of priorities for combined SC partnering in third countries.

We further identified mitigation strategies that could help overcome some of these barriers. These mitigation strategies present various levels of complexity that, in some cases, can make their implementation challenging, often requiring other parts of DoD and even the U.S. State Department to resolve. With only 11 case studies and an emphasis on depth over breadth, we have to be cautious about drawing broad conclusions and making specific recommendations. Still, our research pointed to a few key areas in which action would allow the DAF to make significant advances in the short term to address some of the pervasive barriers noted in our research.

We focus here on four key priority strategies that present the highest potential payoff for the Secretary of the Air Force for International Affairs (SAF/IA) and, by extension, the DAF. The strategies were selected according to the following factors:

1. They can be implemented by the United States and are not dependent on actions undertaken by allies and partners.
2. They can be implemented largely by SAF/IA, or SAF/IA and a limited number of other DAF/DoD organizations that SAF/IA works closely with.
3. They cover a large number of the mitigation strategies suggested by our case studies, either within a single domain or across domains.

The following points focus mainly on manpower and expertise, streamlining communication with allies and partners, and improving information-sharing platforms.

First, **the DAF and allies and partners would benefit from a review of the legal authorities for the roles and the placement of exchanges, nonreciprocal exchanges, and liaison officers (LNOs), many of which are legacy positions**. Information-sharing challenges were a recurrent theme throughout our case studies. Increasing bilateral defense exchanges in research, development, testing, and evaluation and in cooperative development to improve coordination and understanding of expectations, capabilities, and needs could help address these challenges, but there are legal issues pertaining to what sensitive information exchange officers can share with their home country and the levels of classification that LNOs can typically have access to. Although this strategy would require some policy changes (and, potentially, changes to U.S. law), it might be worth exploring a new hybrid status between exchange officer and LNO positions that would allow for more information-sharing with highly capable allies and partners within set limits. A review of legacy positions could also help determine which ones might be discontinued in favor of more-impactful future positions.

Second, **given the increase in demand for technical expertise in new and growing SC domains (space, cyber), it would be helpful to ensure that the foreign disclosure community is enabled with sufficient technical or domain-specific expertise** (and embedded in the relevant organizations) to make rapid decisions. Because of the services' funding constraints for new manpower requirements, it will be critical to engage the Defense Security Cooperation Agency on this issue to approve Foreign Military Sales funding for additional foreign disclosure positions. Space- and cyber-specific disclosure policy and corresponding security classification guidance would increase the benefit realized from the proposed infusion of needed disclosure expertise and capacity.

Third, **it would be useful to look for ways for the DAF to improve its advocacy for the inclusion of international equities throughout a program's life cycle**. This could include the identification of a DAF "champion" for each major U.S. capability development initiative to improve transparency and accountability internally and streamline communications with highly capable allies and partners. Ensuring timely senior leader (within and outside the DAF) attention on issues for which there is internal U.S. government disagreement (e.g., security-related risk tolerance) could help reduce the friction from the complex, distributed U.S. system. In more concrete terms, DAF leadership could initiate a review of major acquisition programs in which highly capable allies and partners are involved to ensure there is (1) a single office point of contact and a single coordinating authority to lead negotiations and (2) a communication strategy in place for the more complex and more sensitive programs for which allies and partners do not have full access. Further efforts to reduce U.S. complexity, which can be daunting for allies and partners, could include centralizing functions where practical (e.g., creating a joint terminal program for operations or a single point of contact for partners for space SC).

Fourth, **the DAF would benefit from supporting additional allied and partner access to collaborative platforms to facilitate cooperation and information-sharing**. Cyber cooperation, in particular, could benefit from such efforts. This could include developing secure collaborative infrastructure between the United States and partner cyber organizations to discuss issues that may be unclassified for the United States but classified for partners (or the other way around). More broadly, this could increase the information security community's role in working with allies and partners to (1) develop a shared understanding of what is sensitive and (2) establish security controls that protect the information in a way that meets cyber community operational needs and addresses U.S. intelligence and technology protection concerns. In the cyber domain, ways to overcome recurrent information-sharing issues might include investing in collaborative infrastructure that uses artificial intelligence–enabled authentication and access (zero-trust environments) rather than hardware workarounds (Battlefield Information Collection and Exploitation System [BICES] terminals, SIPRNet Releasable [SIPR REL], etc.).

In this report, we link the mitigation strategies with the relevant stakeholder communities that the DAF would work with to problem-solve together. We suggest the DAF focus mostly on the options intended to improve SC planning and that senior DAF leadership focus on improving coordination and communication among the various stakeholder communities. We recognize that some of the mitigation strategies are easier to implement than others and that the more difficult ones are worthy of further study and analysis to determine the most appropriate way ahead.

Contents

Figures and Tables

Figures

Tables

Chapter 1. Introduction

Study Scope and Research Questions

The Department of the Air Force (DAF), like the entire U.S. Department of Defense (DoD), has been directed to support the 2022 National Defense Strategy, which prioritizes defending the homeland and deterring attacks against the United States and its allies and partners. The National Defense Strategy emphasizes that mutually beneficial alliances and partnerships are an enduring strength for the United States and are critical to achieving U.S. objectives. It calls on DoD to incorporate ally and partner perspectives, competencies, and advantages at every stage of defense planning.[3]

Highly capable U.S. allies and partners have much to offer in these efforts. *Highly capable* allies and partners are those with deep capability and experience in one or more of the domains of air, space, and cyber. The United Kingdom (UK), for example, would be a highly capable U.S. ally in all three domains, whereas Estonia would be a highly capable U.S. ally in cyber only. Highly capable allies and partners have regional and country expertise, deployment experience, logistics understanding, and intelligence from relationships that complement U.S. knowledge. In short, they can play a central role by providing forces, access, intelligence, technology, and legitimacy to U.S.-led operations. They also have innovative capabilities and approaches to working with additional partners.

The character and nature of security cooperation (SC) with highly capable allies and partners differs in many respects from the efforts to develop nascent air, space, or cyber capabilities. Some U.S. cooperation activities, such as the co-development and co-production of new capabilities; research, development, testing, and evaluation (RDT&E); and the sharing of sophisticated technologies, only take place with highly capable partners. The ability of the United States to develop synergies with and leverage its highly capable allies could help it maintain a favorable global balance of power and enhance its ability to develop cutting-edge technologies and opportunities for interoperability. Highly capable allies and partners tend to have historic, well-established SC with the United States, but pursuing new capabilities with them can still pose challenges. Co-development and co-production of new capabilities, particularly those regarding sensitive technology and information, can require complex (even novel) financial, scientific, and industrial agreements.

Therefore, although highly capable allies and partners are often positioned to cooperate with the United States across air, space, and cyber domains, many barriers can prevent the achievement of shared strategic objectives and the development of the capacity to dominate these

---

[3] DoD, "Fact Sheet: 2022 National Defense Strategy," March 28, 2022.

domains. These barriers include overly restrictive information-sharing policies, insufficient involvement in each other's planning processes, a lack of understanding of each other's SC processes and regional and country focus areas, and unrealized capability co-development and co-production opportunities that could otherwise promote interoperability.

In this report, we consider the ways and means by which the DAF and DoD can enhance engagement with highly capable allies and partners by exploring the following key questions:

- What are the main strategic benefits and risks to collaborating with highly capable allies and partners, including in third countries, from *both* a U.S. and an allied or partner perspective (Chapter 1)?
- What types of barriers exist (Chapter 2)?
- How do these types of barriers manifest in specific SC programs and activities (Chapter 3)?
- What options exist to mitigate some of these barriers (Chapters 3 and 4)?

In this volume, we provide an overview of our approach and identify domain-specific and cross-domain barriers across 11 case studies, as well as potential mitigation strategies. A second volume provides a similar overview, as well as the detail of the 11 case studies.[4]

Collaboration with Highly Capable Allies and Partners Comes with Enormous Benefits but also Risks

DoD SC with highly capable allies and partners, such as the UK, Australia, and Japan (as well as those with advanced niche capabilities, such as India and Estonia), is ubiquitous but involves a distinct set of benefits and objectives—as well as activities and risks—that differ, often significantly, from those of most U.S. and DAF partners. The 2022 National Defense Strategy emphasizes working with "our unmatched network of alliances and partnerships" to implement integrated deterrence and "develop our own warfighting capabilities together with Allies and partners."[5]

Federal guidance suggests several priorities for engagement with highly capable allies and partners. U.S. decisionmakers must consider these priorities and benefits as they weigh different levels of collaboration. These priorities and benefits include the following:

- *Deepening cooperation, interoperability, and integration* to enable combined forces to act together coherently and effectively to achieve military objectives and become more integrated with the Joint Force.

---

[4] Jennifer D. P. Moroney, Stephanie Pezard, David E. Thaler, Gene Germanovich, Beth Grill, Bruce McClintock, Karen Schwindt, Mary Kate Adgie, Anika Binnendijk, Kevin J. Connolly, Katie Feistel, Jeffrey W. Hornung, Alison K. Hottes, Moon Kim, Isabelle Nazha, Gabrielle Tarini, Mark Toukan, and Jalen Zeman, *Overcoming Barriers to Working with Highly Capable Allies and Partners in the Air, Space, and Cyber Domains: Case Studies*, Santa Monica, Calif.: RAND Corporation, RR-A968-2, 2023, Not available to the general public.

[5] DoD, 2022, p. 2.

- *Investing in a common defense architecture* to allow allies and partners to pool resources and share responsibility for the common defense. For the cyber domain, a common defense architecture is not necessarily applicable, but investing together in cyber defense is appropriate.
- *Modernizing key capabilities to create a more lethal and innovative combined force,* which includes cooperating with highly capable allies to modernize nuclear forces; space-based capabilities; cyber capabilities; command, control, communications, computers, intelligence, surveillance, and reconnaissance; missile defense and strike; and autonomous capabilities.
- *Contributing to the development of operational concepts* to deter and win a high-end fight and concepts for organizing and employing forces for highly contested environments.
- *Maintaining and expanding access* to provide strategic flexibility and freedom of action. This includes access to critical regions and widespread basing and logistics systems that underpin DoD's global reach. (Access is not applicable to collaboration in the cyber domain.)
- *Shoring up regional alliances, increasing influence in great-power competition, and establishing norms,* for which allies can provide complementary capabilities and distinct perspectives, regional relationships, and information that improves the U.S. understanding of the environment and expands U.S. options.[6]

Thus, U.S. defense collaboration with allies and partners is a critical pillar of national security and defense strategy. Such collaboration enables the United States to pursue its most vital national interests around the globe. But SC comes with risks. U.S. decisionmakers may, for strategic, geopolitical, relationship, or other reasons, assign different levels of risk to collaboration with various highly capable allies and partners. They must consider risks associated with internationalizing the supply chain for U.S. military capabilities and equipment, sharing sensitive information with partners that have different standards and practices, losing control of intellectual property, and the possibility of industrial espionage as they weigh collaboration with different countries.

The need to minimize risk has propelled Congress and the Departments of State and Defense to formulate laws, regulations, bureaucracies, and processes regarding potential threats to U.S. national security that can arise through close collaboration with foreign nations. These efforts to safeguard national security can also create barriers that inhibit smooth collaboration with even the closest allies. These barriers are a by-product of the trade-offs the United States must make between the benefits and risks of cooperation with foreign nations. In this report, we seek to

---

[6] See DoD, *Summary of the 2018 National Defense Strategy of the United States: Sharpening the American Military's Competitive Edge,* Washington, D.C., 2018b; DoD, *Summary: Department of Defense Cyber Strategy 2018,* Washington, D.C., 2018a; and DoD, *Defense Space Strategy,* Washington, D.C., June 2020. See also The White House, *Interim National Security Strategic Guidance,* Washington, D.C., March 2021; Joint Chiefs of Staff, *The National Military Strategy of the United States of America,* Washington, D.C., June 2015; and DoD, *Sustaining U.S. Global Leadership: Priorities for 21st Century Defense,* Washington, D.C., January 2012.

understand these barriers and identify areas where they might be reduced to enable deepened collaboration without greatly increasing risk.

Research Approach

Our study had two main tasks. First, we reviewed research on benefits and risks for the United States in regard to cooperating with allies and partners, with special attention paid to highly capable allies and partners. Although there is extensive work on the benefits and risks of alliances in general, there is little research on barriers to SC with highly capable allies and partners,[7] with research regarding barriers in the air, space, and cyber domains more limited still. Most insights we found on barriers to collaborating with allies and partners were in the form of anecdotes. As a result, we had to rely heavily on targeted interviews with U.S. and allied or partner officials, as well as with other specialists outside of government who have direct experience working together.

Second, using our team's SC expertise, we developed criteria to select case studies. These criteria included domains, regions, type of partner or ally, and type of SC program or activity. Working closely with the Secretary of the Air Force for International Affairs (SAF/IA), we selected 11 case studies across the air, space, and cyber domains.[8] We selected cases of *steady-state* SC—i.e., excluding collaboration during military operations—that involved barriers that we identified during our research. We selected particularly complex (and interesting) cases—many of which included elements of sales, reinforcing exercises, co-development and co-production, and senior personnel exchanges.

---

[7] Our literature review found no study on barriers in general but rather found more-specific studies on gaps and challenges related to specific objectives or bilateral relations. See, for instance, Christopher G. Pernin, Jakub P. Hlavka, Matthew E. Boyer, John Gordon IV, Michael Lerario, Jan Osburg, Michael Shurkin, and Daniel C. Gibson, *Targeted Interoperability: A New Imperative for Multinational Operations*, Santa Monica, Calif.: RAND Corporation, RR-2075-A, 2019; Thomas W. Ross, "Enhancing Security Cooperation Effectiveness: A Model for Capability Package Planning," *Joint Force Quarterly*, No. 80, January 2016; Andrus W. Chaney, "Implementing Guidance for Security Cooperation: Overcoming Obstacles to U.S. Africa Command's Efforts," *Joint Force Quarterly*, No. 88, 1st Quarter 2018; Terrence Kelly, Jefferson P. Marquis, Cathryn Quantic Thurston, Jennifer D. P. Moroney, and Charlotte Lynch, *Security Cooperation Organizations in the Country Team: Options for Success*, Santa Monica, Calif.: RAND Corporation, TR-734-A, 2010; Kristina Obecny and Gregory Sanders, *U.S.-Canadian Defense Industrial Cooperation*, Washington, D.C.: Center for Strategic and International Studies, June 2017; and Rachel Hoff, "Next Steps for U.S.-Japan Security Cooperation," Sasakawa USA, June 8, 2016. Some studies also highlight challenges that are internal to DoD and might have an impact on working with allies and partners, even though this is not the specific focus of these studies. See, for instance, Jessie Riposo, Megan McKernan, Jeffrey A. Drezner, Geoffrey McGovern, Daniel Tremblay, Jason Kumar, and Jerry M. Sollinger, *Issues with Access to Acquisition Data and Information in the Department of Defense: Executive Summary*, Santa Monica, Calif.: RAND Corporation, RR-880/1-OSD, 2015; and Bolko J. Skorupski and Nina M. Serafino, *DOD Security Cooperation: An Overview of Authorities and Issues*, Washington, D.C.: Congressional Research Service, R44602, August 23, 2016.

[8] See Chapter 4 for case study selection criteria and details of the 11 cases.

Because of coronavirus disease 2019 (COVID-19) pandemic restrictions, we selected cases for which we could conduct interviews remotely. Our goal of publishing an unclassified report further restricted our choice of cases, as did our goal to identify cases in which barriers had been overcome. Because our research had to rely on interviews, we also sought relatively recent cases (i.e., within the past ten years) for which interviewees were likely to have a better memory of specifics. We focused on cases of high strategic priority, as well as those of substantial DAF investment: that is, those that brought together diverse U.S. and ally and partner organizations, required high funding levels, and had an extended time frame.

We selected case studies to cover the air, space, and cyber domains. We also selected them to represent different types of engagements, including at least one multinational collaborative effort and at least two combatant command areas of responsibility. We selected case studies both inside and outside the Five Eyes (FVEY) group, composed of the United States, the UK, Australia, Canada, and New Zealand. We selected cases that represented various SC activities, including SC activities in cooperation with an allied country in a third country.

To identify SC activities to cover in our case studies, we drew from activities that the DAF conducts with highly capable allies from among all the activities associated with SC "categories" in Joint Publication 3-20 (*Security Cooperation*) and SC "tools" in SAF/IA's *International Engagement Plan*.[9] The specific categories of activities that we considered were

- *defense and military contacts*, including key leader engagements, subject-matter expert exchanges, staff talks, and conferences
- *standing forums*, including institutionalized and continuously operating bilateral or multilateral forums, such as the Air Force Interoperability Council
- *personnel exchanges* of U.S. and allied airmen to each other's defense organizations for extended detail
- *exercises*, both tabletop and live, with large military formations and multiple mission sets
- *combined training* of U.S. and allied airmen on common systems and procedures
- *education* of U.S. and foreign airmen at each other's professional military education institutions and war colleges
- *international armaments cooperation*, including co-development, co-production, cooperative production, licensed production, and combined RDT&E efforts
- *sales*, including Foreign Military Sales and direct commercial sales, which may also include co-production and licensed production
- *information and intelligence exchanges* of sensitive information for mutual benefit
- *access, basing, overflight, and Status of Forces Agreements*, which enable the presence of defense assets in allied countries (this category excludes many other agreements that enable other SC activities)
- *cooperative logistics* for acquisition, exercises, and operations

---

[9] See Joint Publication 3-20, *Security Cooperation*, Washington, D.C.: Joint Chiefs of Staff, May 23, 2017, pp. III-14–III-15; and SAF/IA, *Department of the Air Force International Engagement Plan*, Washington, D.C., July 2020, pp. 7–8.

- *planning and coordination in third countries or combined SC* (the preparation and execution with allies of combined SC efforts in other countries in pursuit of mutual interests).

Ultimately, we selected 11 cases—five in the air domain, three in the space domain, and three in the cyber domain—as shown in Figure 1.1.

Figure 1.1. Eleven Case Studies Across Three Domains

AIR	SPACE	CYBER
ABMS: Australia, UK	WGS: multiple allies and partners	AUSTRALIA
Wedgetail: Australia, UK	Arctic military SATCOM: Norway	ESTONIA
Defense Technology and Trade Initiative (Air-launched UAV): India	Quasi-Zenith Satellite System: Japan	FINLAND
F-35 Co-production: Italy		
"Combined SC Partnering" (collaborating with allies in third countries)		

NOTE: ABMS = Advanced Battle Management System; SATCOM = satellite communications; UAV = unmanned aerial vehicle; WGS = Wideband Global SATCOM.

These cases covered a wide range of SC activities: RDT&E, exercises, information- and intelligence-sharing, high-level and personnel exchanges, standing forums, Foreign Military Sales, direct commercial sales, planning and coordination in third countries, and cooperative development. Many of these activities are most common in relations between the United States and its most highly capable allies and partners, because they involve the development and sharing of advanced, sensitive technologies. The only two types of SC activities we did not cover were (1) access and basing agreements and (2) cooperative logistics (e.g., Acquisition and Cross Servicing Agreements) because of time and resource constraints. We matched these SC activities with the types of barriers that the case studies illustrate (Figure 1.2). Although the cases do not include all barriers that might manifest in SC activities, we believe this set provides sufficient coverage to illustrate the complexities of SC. Figure 1.2 also shows that the most prevalent barriers we found in our cases are cultural, bureaucratic, and budgetary.

Figure 1.2. Crosswalk of Security Cooperation Activities in Case Studies with Types of Barriers

		Type of barrier						
		Budgetary	Bureaucratic	Cultural	Political	Regulatory	Strategic	Technical
SC Activities	Research, Development, Test, and Evaluation (RDT&E)	X	X	X	X	X	X	X
	Exercises	X	X	X				X
	Information/Intelligence Sharing		X	X		X		X
	High-level and personnel exchanges	X	X	X		X		X
	Standing forums (e.g., AFIC), ad hoc meetings			X				
	FMS	X	X					
	DCS			X				
	Cooperative development (e.g., co-development, co-production)	X	X	X	X	X	X	X
	Access & basing agreements							
	Cooperative logistics (e.g., ACSAs)							

NOTE: ACSA = Acquisition and Cross Servicing Agreement; AFIC = Air Force Interoperability Council; DCS = direct commercial sales; FMS = Foreign Military Sales.

Our sources for the case studies included primary and secondary sources in English and Japanese, as well as 104 interviews with U.S. (75) and foreign (29) officials and defense experts. All three domain-focused teams obtained key data and insights from interviews, allowing for domain-specific and cross-domain analysis and findings. Our small sample size of 11 case studies limits the generalizability of our observations and the mitigation strategies derived from them. Nevertheless, the addition of a few more cases (maybe focused on one barrier, one ally or partner, or one type of activity) may allow generalizability.

Overall, the literature reviews allowed us to build a typology of barriers, and the case studies gave us a chance to test the utility of this typology and provided specific examples of how these types of barriers manifest. The literature review on the benefits and risks to cooperating, as well as the barriers and potential mitigation strategies identified in the case studies, form the basis of our recommendations for the DAF. Figure 1.3 outlines our approach and this report's organization.

Figure 1.3. Research Approach and Report Organization

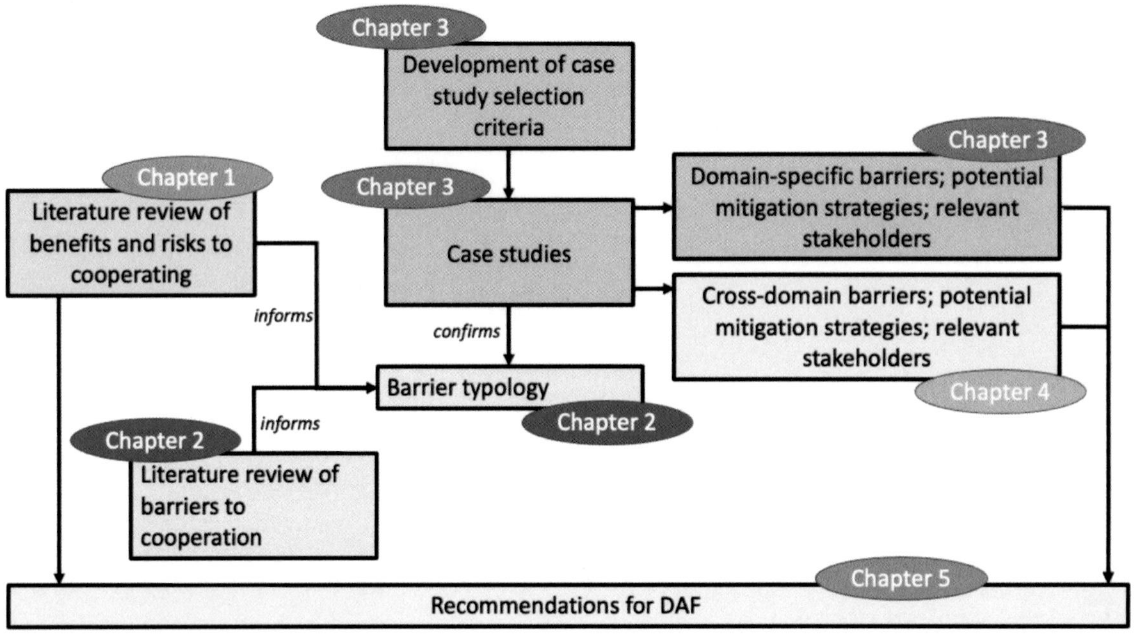

In Chapter 2, we tackle the questions of barriers to working with highly capable allies and partners and present the barriers typology that we use for the analysis. In Chapter 3, we provide an overview of our case studies and domain-specific barriers drawn from the case studies. Chapter 3 includes a series of potential mitigation strategies and the stakeholder communities that could be involved in addressing these barriers. In Chapter 4, we present seven cross-domain barriers, along with potential mitigation strategies and relevant stakeholder communities. In Chapter 5, we conclude the report with a discussion about easier to implement actions that the DAF could take, as well as a brief discussion about good practices for working with allies and partners. We wrap up Chapter 5 with a few ideas of where next to take this exploratory research.

Overall, we find the following:

- Many barriers are interconnected, adding complexity to both the problem and solution.
- Some mitigation strategies could be implemented by SAF/IA and A5, while others need to be implemented by DAF leadership or external organizations within DoD.
- Some mitigation strategies can be described as "low-hanging fruit," while others might be more difficult to address: requiring, for example, changes to International Traffic in Arms Regulations (ITAR) regarding technology the United States acquires that originates in foreign countries.
- For barriers originating with the ally or partner, the most important mitigation strategies would be an early assessment of where frictions might exist, so that they can be accounted for in program planning.
- There appear to be few examples in which collaborating with allies in a third country has worked.

Chapter 2. Examples of Barriers to Successful Collaboration with Highly-Capable Allies and Partners

As discussed in Chapter 1, SC with highly capable allies and partners brings many benefits—including enhanced interoperability, burden-sharing, and signaling alliance cohesion to adversaries—but also entails risks and drawbacks. In this chapter, we present and then unpack our typology on barriers to collaborating with highly capable allies and partners. We refined this typology several times as we learned more from the case study analysis. The typology, plus the findings from the cases in Chapter 3, are intended to help move the conversation among DoD, DAF, and key allied and partner officials from anecdotes to evidence and to better understand the impact of the most pervasive and recurring barriers that hinder U.S. and allied or partner collaboration.

New Typology for Reviewing and Categorizing Security Cooperation Barriers

The United States may face a variety of barriers that hinder SC with its highly capable allies and partners. Such barriers would affect not only the willingness of the United States and its partners to cooperate but also their capabilities to do so. That is, these barriers may make partnering more difficult, less beneficial, or even impossible. The barriers can be country-specific, such as U.S. legal restrictions on sharing information or the domestic political interests of its ally or partner. The barriers can also stem from general differences between the United States and its ally or partner, such as misaligned financial resources or incompatible technological platforms.

The literature on barriers to SC is sparse, and the literature on barriers that are specific to highly capable allies is even more limited. The available research on this topic was largely anecdotal and specific to the partner cooperating with the United States. This literature gap further emphasizes the importance of more broadly considering SC barriers using historical evidence. Several of the risks highlighted above are at the root of why SC is not always a straightforward process. Protecting oneself against these risks requires some checks, regulations, and levels of oversight that can delay or otherwise impede some activities. In other words, the United States—as well as its allies and partners—put in place several barriers to prevent these risks from negatively affecting its security and strategic objectives.

Using our review of the available literature, we identified seven overall categories of barriers. In this report, we classify the types of barriers that may affect SC with highly capable partners as budgetary, regulatory, bureaucratic, cultural, political, technical, and strategic. In some cases, these barriers seek to prevent the risks highlighted above, although they may not match exactly (i.e., one barrier will not necessarily address one risk). For instance, risks related to information-sharing are routinely mitigated through regulatory, technical, and bureaucratic barriers. In other cases, barriers are not safeguards but rather inefficiencies produced by bureaucratic differences, political friction, strategic divergence, or other challenges that creep into SC activities between the United States and its most capable allies and partners to create delays or, in the worst-case scenario, prevent them from achieving their objectives.

Budgetary Barriers

Cooperation requires a financial commitment from the United States and its partners, but the financial resources and priorities of the countries may not align. The United States or its partner could have distinct funding authorities (with specific parameters and restrictions) that must be harmonized prior to cooperation. The United States and its partners will need to ensure their cooperation is financially viable, which can be a challenge, given the vast U.S. defense budget relative to other countries. In some cases, budgetary limitations come from the United States. In 2013, for instance, Congress blocked the U.S. contribution to the Medium Extended Air Defense System, triggering complaints from program partners Italy and Germany.[10] In addition to differences in funding priorities or the availability of resources, the United States and its allies and partners may struggle with determining the fair share of costing requirements.

Regulatory Barriers

U.S. regulatory barriers can include written prohibitions or limitations to collaboration in legal code, legislation, or departmental instructions. Possible restrictions can include sharing of intelligence and export or import restrictions of defense material. Ally or partner regulatory barriers can include legal or executive-level restrictions on collaboration with foreign partners. For instance, defense engagement between Japan and the United States increased only after Japan relaxed its constitutional prohibition to using military force and took several actions that included creating a National Security Council, modifying its arms exports policies, and increasing defense spending.[11] Other legal restrictions may affect specific types of cooperation, including defense industrial cooperation. U.S. foreign acquisition restrictions, such as the Berry Amendment and the Byrnes-Tollefson Amendment, and export control policies can severely complicate cooperation by limiting the exchange of technical data and information.[12] Even though Canada has an "exemption" from the export controls of ITAR, legal barriers still exist for

---

[10] "Germany, Italy Protest at U.S Axing of Missile Defense Funding," Reuters, February 2, 2013.

[11] Hoff, 2016.

[12] Obecny and Sanders, 2017.

it, even more so for other countries pursuing defense industrial cooperation with the United States.[13]

Bureaucratic Barriers

Cooperation between the United States and its allies and partners means navigating each country's distinct bureaucratic processes and requirements. Bureaucratic challenges that could impede cooperation include personnel turnover, coordination and scheduling difficulties, over-classification of communications (defaulting to Not Releasable to Foreign Nationals, or NOFORN), and conflicting priorities and incentives within U.S. and partner organizations. The sheer number of stakeholders and organizations involved in a single SC program can slow communication and decisions, particularly if the program is new or complex. Partners and allies may also need to harmonize unsynchronized planning and funding cycles. Greater coordination can help overcome these barriers, and addressing these challenges early on at the various echelons is recommended.[14] One such example is U.S. Army Africa inviting British army personnel to participate in its annual order and multiyear planning cycles.[15]

Cultural Barriers

Proper understanding or acknowledgment of the cultural and historic conditions related to the participating countries is a valuable element of successful cooperation. Even with aligned priorities and technical platforms, partners may still struggle to effectively cooperate if they have their own cultural norms and terminologies, and their native languages may differ. Cultural barriers might also include differing approaches or expectations regarding military cooperation and different understandings of what constitutes sensitive or classified data. Experience in bilateral or multilateral engagements might facilitate SC activities but will not always do so. A review of the Trilateral Strategic Initiative, a cooperation effort between the U.S., French, and British air forces found that, despite these allies' long history of cooperation, each still tends to fall back on "cultural reflexes towards national solutions" rather than working together and adopting a "more trilateral perspective."[16] Translation and communication issues were a primary barrier to success between the UK and France during a joint expeditionary exercise.[17]

---

[13] Obecny and Sanders, 2017.

[14] Pernin et al., 2019.

[15] Chaney, 2018, p. 96.

[16] Peter Goldfein and André Adamson, "The Trilateral Strategic Initiative: A Primer for Developing Future Airpower Cooperation," *Air & Space Power Journal*, Vol. 30, No. 4, Winter 2016, p. 79.

[17] Goldfein and Adamson, 2016, p. 78.

Political Barriers

Political barriers include governmental restrictions or limitations that are external to DoD or the ally's or partner's defense ministry. They can come from domestic pressures or influences from industry, legislatures, or popular opinion and, in some cases, negatively affect U.S. engagement efforts. In Japan, some have expressed concern that closer security ties with the United States pull Japan into an "Iraq War-style adventure."[18] Protectionist tendencies of domestic industrial bases could also be a concern, as in Japan and Australia, where

> a great deal of apprehension exists that their industries will become mere subsidiaries of major U.S. defense firms in international joint development and production of defense equipment, supplying parts and components rather than developing high-value technology.[19]

Other national concerns may come into play, such as when the United States threatened to scale back intelligence-sharing with Germany if Huawei, a Chinese telecommunications company, was permitted to build its mobile-internet infrastructure in Germany.[20] The United States may face difficulties when tensions arise between partners, as they have between South Korea and Japan, complicating the U.S. goal of cooperating multilaterally.[21]

Technical Barriers

Technological incompatibility and a lack of interoperability can be a prevalent barrier for SC.[22] Technical barriers range from a lack of compatible systems or procedures for sharing information to imbalances in scientific or domain expertise. In some cases, the United States may lack confidence in the ability of an ally or partner to effectively protect classified or sensitive information. Technical barriers have been seen in exercises. In 2019, U.S., British, and French air forces participated in the Point Blank exercise, and although the forces were interoperable, communication between pilots of more-advanced aircraft suffered because of incompatibilities with the Link-16 network.[23] Furthermore, the U.S. prioritization of technological development and advancement places a burden on its allies to "keep up," which could ultimately affect their

---

[18] Hoff, 2016, p. 13.

[19] Yuki Tatsumi, "US-Japan-Australia Cooperation in Defense Equipment: Untapped Potential or a Bridge Too Far?" in Yuki Tatsumi, ed., *US-Japan-Australia Security Cooperation: Prospects and Challenges*, Washington, D.C.: Stimson Center, April 2015b, p. 85.

[20] Bojan Pancevski and Sara Germano, "Drop Huawei or See Intelligence Sharing Pared Back, U.S. Tells Germany," *Wall Street Journal*, March 11, 2019.

[21] Gudrun Wacker, *Security Cooperation in East Asia: Structures, Trends and Limitations*, Berlin: German Institute for International and Security Affairs, May 2015.

[22] Pernin et al., 2019.

[23] Anika Binnendijk, Gene Germanovich, Bruce McClintock, and Sarah Heintz, *At the Vanguard: European Contributions to NATO's Future Combat Airpower*, Santa Monica, Calif.: RAND Corporation, RR-A311-1, 2020.

willingness and ability to cooperate with the United States.[24] The use of differing technologies can also make cooperation difficult or impossible. For example, Turkey's purchase of a Russian S-400 air-defense missile system led the United States to "unwind" Turkey from the F-35 program, given security and intelligence concerns that the United States saw a Russian system posing to the program.[25]

Strategic Barriers

Even close allies can have diverging high-level priorities and views regarding domestic and global security, threat perceptions, approaches to security, and other strategic issues.[26] For example, although the United States may identify China as a growing security threat and global competitor, other countries may not view China the same way. They may therefore be less likely to engage in security activities that counter China.[27] Similarly, although France supports "direct" military intervention against violent extremist organizations in West Africa, the United States favors an "indirect" approach.[28] In addition, "France's preference for unilateralism in West Africa has restricted its ability to work with Washington on developing a regional security strategy."[29] Finally, New Zealand's staunch anti–nuclear weapons policies restricted its military cooperation with the United States, though the two countries have steadily addressed this barrier.[30]

Conclusion

Table 2.1 summarizes the seven types of barriers we identified and offers representative examples of each. Some extenuating events, such as the COVID-19 pandemic, manifested as a variety of barriers that could be included in these categories. The pandemic, for example, and the resulting shift to virtual communications, emphasized technical barriers, whereas the closure of

---

[24] Pernin et al., 2019.

[25] Jim Garamone, "U.S. Begins Process of 'Unwinding' Turkey from F-35 Program, DoD Officials Say," U.S. Department of Defense, July 17, 2019.

[26] Jennifer D. P. Moroney, Celeste Ward Gventer, Stephanie Pezard, and Laurence Smallman, *Lessons from U.S. Allies in Security Cooperation with Third Countries: The Cases of Australia, France, and the United Kingdom*, Santa Monica, Calif.: RAND Corporation, TR-972-AF, 2011.

[27] Yuki Tatsumi, "Introduction" in Yuki Tatsumi, ed., *US-Japan-Australia Security Cooperation: Prospects and Challenges*, Washington, D.C.: Stimson Center, April 2015a.

[28] Stephen F. Burgess, "Military Intervention in Africa: French and US Approaches Compared," *Journal of European, Middle Eastern, and African Affairs*, Vol. 1, No. 1, Spring 2019.

[29] Samuel Ramani, "France and the United States Are Making West Africa's Security Situation Worse," *Foreign Policy*, September 12, 2020.

[30] Rob Taylor, "U.S., New Zealand End Rift over Nuclear-Weapons Policies," *Wall Street Journal*, July 21, 2016.

ports or limited access to U.S. air bases illustrated political and strategic barriers.[31] There are other circumstances not captured in these categories that can pose additional barriers.

Table 2.1. Barriers Typology

Type of Barrier	Representative examples
Budgetary	• Differences in funding priorities or availability of resources • Inability to determine or agree to fair share (costing requirements)
Bureaucratic	• Sheer number of stakeholders and organizations • Over-classification of communications (default to NOFORN) • Conflicting priorities and incentives within U.S. and partner organizations
Cultural	• Differing approaches or expectations regarding military cooperation • Reluctance or inability to share sensitive or classified data • Historical experience in bilateral or multilateral engagements/relationships
Political	• Governmental restrictions or limitations external to DoD or MoD • Domestic pressures or influences from industry, legislatures, or popular opinion
Regulatory	• Written prohibitions or limitations to collaboration in U.S. legal code, Congressional legislation, or departmental instructions • Ally/partner legal or executive-level restrictions on collaboration with foreign partners
Strategic	• Diverging national interests and threat perceptions • Differences in priorities re: collaboration with U.S. and other allies and partners
Technical	• Lack of compatible systems or procedures to share information • Imbalances in scientific or domain expertise • Lack of confidence in ally/partner's ability to protect effectively classified or sensitive information

NOTE: MoD = Ministry of Defense.

We find that these barriers are rarely independent of one another. For instance, political issues, such as domestic pressures on an ally's or partner's leadership, can lead to regulatory changes that limit the types or extent of activities that can be carried out. Limited information-sharing can be the result of multiple other barriers. The extent to which the United States can share information with its allies and partners is a regulatory barrier, but often it is the bureaucratic practice of adopting a conservative interpretation of the regulation and overusing the NOFORN classification that limits collaboration most. In some cases, the lack of a platform to exchange information safely is a technical issue. In others, communications are hampered by a lack of trust among partners—a cultural barrier that may reflect a nascent SC relationship.

According to this literature review, it is unclear whether U.S. relations with some subcategories of highly capable allies and partners might be more prone to specific types of barriers. We would expect some of the barriers associated with information-sharing (such as political, cultural, and technical barriers) to be less prevalent between the United States and other FVEY countries than with others. However, the literature review also shows, somewhat counterintuitively, that cultural issues arise between countries that have a long history of working

---

[31] Sara Sirota, "Air Force Confronting Defense Cooperation Challenges with Allies During COVID-19," *Inside Defense*, April 28, 2020.

together, such as the United States, the UK, and France, and that strategic barriers can arise even when the United States and its ally (in this case, France) share the same strategic objective (countering violent extremism in West Africa). More broadly, the paucity of the literature on barriers makes it difficult to have a granular view of how they apply (or whether they apply differently) to specific categories of highly capable allies and partners. Case studies, however, may provide that additional level of granularity. The following chapter delves into detail on the case studies we conducted across the air, space, and cyber domains and includes a discussion of the cases in the context of the types of barriers we identified in this chapter.

Chapter 3. Selection and Summaries of Air, Space, and Cyber Case Studies

In this chapter, we present summaries of the 11 case studies. Although our cases are broadly representative of the different barriers and SC activities, we do not claim to have uncovered and assessed all possible barriers to collaborating with highly capable allies and partners. Instead, we offer these insights as a starting point for future research.

Our case studies illustrate the barriers that have, at times, slowed or impeded SC programs, even in instances in which such programs were considered a priority, such as for ABMS. These cases show that SC is not an easy activity: It requires high levels of coordination and a keen ability to adapt processes to individual programs and relationships, especially for complex or novel programs. We describe our findings and potential mitigation strategies within individual domains in this chapter and discuss cross-domain findings and mitigation strategies in Chapter 4.

Given the limited number of cases, we cannot make inferences on how widespread a specific challenge or barrier might be. For instance, a challenge found in only one of our three space cases might turn out to be highly common.

For each finding, we point to one or more mitigation strategies that have been attempted or suggested. Again, the limited number of cases prevents inferences regarding the likelihood that a given mitigation strategy will succeed. Although our cases might only show failures for a given strategy, such a strategy might succeed elsewhere.

To facilitate implementation, we also identify the key stakeholder communities that would be involved in the proposed mitigation strategies. The space and cyber domains have their distinct communities of interest, but the air domain, which is more varied, does not. We sought advice from SAF/IA on these categories, and our list casts a wide net on those across DoD and the DAF who work with allies and partners. The stakeholder communities, and examples of organizations and offices within those communities, include the following:

- **Concept Formulation and Development.** DAF Rapid Capabilities Offices, Chief Architect Office, Air Force Futures Office.
- **Foreign Disclosure.** Director of Security, Special Program Oversight and Information Protection (SAF/AAZ); Defense Technology Security Agency.
- **Information Security.** DAF Information Security, National Security Agency.
- **Manpower and Training.** DAF A1, Space Force.
- **Operations.** DAF A3O, U.S. Space Command, U.S. Cyber Command, Space Force.
- **Policy and SC Planning.** Secretary of the Air Force for International Affairs Policy and Strategy Directorate, Secretary of the Air Force for International Affairs Regional Affairs Directorate, Air Components, Office of the Under Secretary of Defense for Policy SC, Office of the Under Secretary of Defense for Policy regional and functional (cyber, space) offices, Defense Security Cooperation Agency.

- **Weapons and Acquisition (including science and technology, as well as research and development).** Assistant Secretary of the Air Force for Acquisition, Technology and Logistics; Air Force Research Laboratory, DAF Rapid Capabilities Offices, Office of the Under Secretary of Defense for Acquisition and Sustainment, Space Systems Command.

Our observations may strike some as negative in tone. This is in part because we sought to identify problems associated with current SC practices and processes. We certainly heard from both U.S. and allied and partner officials about great value in every one of these engagements. Nevertheless, to identify possible solutions or mitigation strategies, we focus on problems as the starting point.

Next, we provide an overview of these 11 cases, focusing on the actors, time frame, SC activities, and (most importantly) key challenges regarding SC for each.

Case Studies Overview and Domain-Specific Findings

The following summaries cover our selection of 11 cases. By domain, and in the order we consider them, these cases are

- Air

  - ABMS
  - E-7 Wedgetail
  - Defense Technology and Trade Initiative: Air-Launched UAV
  - F-35 Co-Production with Italy
  - Combined SC Partnering

- Space

  - WGS
  - Arctic Military Satellite Communications System
  - Quasi-Zenith Satellite System (QZSS)

- Cyber

  - U.S.–Australia
  - U.S.–Estonia
  - U.S.–Finland.

Table 3.1 summarizes the barriers associated with each case study. Although these summaries do not convey all the complexities of each case, they outline the key elements that make these cases interesting for identifying ways to overcome SC barriers.

Table 3.1. Barriers, by Case Study

Case Study	Type of Barrier						
	Budgetary	Bureaucratic	Cultural	Political	Regulatory	Strategic	Technical
AIR							
ABMS: Australia, UK		X					X
Wedgetail: Australia, UK	X	X	X		X		X
Air-launched UAV: India	X	X	X	X	X	X	X
F-35 Co-production: Italy				X			
"Combined SC Partnering": collaborating with allies in third countries	X	X	X	X		X	
SPACE							
WGS: multiple allies and partners	X	X	X	X	X		X
Arctic military SATCOM: Norway	X	X	X		X		X
QZSS: Japan		X	X		X	X	X
CYBER							
Australia		X			X	X	X
Estonia	X	X			X	X	X
Finland		X			X	X	X

Air Domain Cases

Advanced Battle Management System

Background

ABMS is the Air Force's main solution for Joint All-Domain Command and Control (JADC2), an evolving concept that addresses how the U.S. military will conduct command and control and maintain a decisionmaking edge in peer and near-peer conflicts.[32] It uses a rapid acquisition framework and a series of technology demonstrations to develop these JADC2-enabling capabilities.[33] Allied involvement to date has been ad hoc and has largely occurred through the JADC2 working group under the Air Force Interoperability Council.[34]

The program began in 2019 and became a program of record in 2020. ABMS has involved personnel exchanges, information-sharing, RDT&E, and the ad hoc use of standing forums with allies and partners. This case highlights some unusual challenges for SC. Given that any high-end conflict would likely be fought alongside allies and partners, ABMS is a high-priority

---

[32] John R. Hoehn, "Joint All-Domain Command and Control: Background and Issues for Congress," Washington, D.C.: Congressional Research Service, R46725, March 18, 2021.

[33] Interview with U.S. defense official, March 2021.

[34] Interview with U.S. defense officials, January 2021.

program.[35] Our case study shows, however, that allies have remained largely outside core ABMS activities to date.[36]

Barriers

We identified several barriers, primarily bureaucratic and technical, to collaboration over ABMS. Bureaucratic barriers have been the most problematic for cooperation, in part because of the complexity and fragmented nature of the program to date. The changing organization and scope of ABMS has made it difficult for allies to understand where to go for information.[37] There has been some confusion within the DAF and DoD as to what the program entails, further complicating collaboration.[38] The default to NOFORN and the lack of network access caused by both technical and bureaucratic challenges has impeded the flow of information to allies. The DAF goal of pursuing ABMS under a rapid acquisition framework may be in tension with the early inclusion of allies in ABMS development.[39] Conflicting priorities and incentives across offices have also posed challenges for collaboration; senior-level guidance stresses the importance of allied involvement, whereas offices involved in program execution include personnel who may not have the background and training to effectively include allies or who perceive sharing information with allies as being riskier than not sharing.[40]

E-7 Wedgetail

Background

The E-7 Wedgetail is the Royal Australian Air Force's airborne early-warning and control platform. It originated in 2000 and achieved initial operational capability for the Royal Australian Air Force in 2012.[41] Although it is largely U.S.-built, it is not in the U.S. inventory.

---

[35] For example, Gen. Jeffrey Harrigan, Commander of U.S. Air Forces Europe, noted that allies must

> be involved in development of concepts and plans, to allow them to decide where and how they can best contribute. You can't just bring them in in execution and go: "Hey we built the plan, so sorry, just do what we told you." (Theresa Hitchens, "Air Force Eyes European ABMS Demo in Spring," *Breaking Defense*, June 29, 2020)

[36] Interview with U.S. defense official, January 2021.

[37] Interview with Australian defense official, April 2021.

[38] Interview with U.S. defense official, March 2021.

[39] Specifically, middle tier acquisition authorities are not recommended for programs that anticipate extensive allied or partnered involvement (Department of Defense Instruction 5000.80, *Operation of the Middle Tier of Acquisition (MTA)*, Washington, D.C.: U.S. Department of Defense, December 30, 2019).

[40] Interviews with U.S. defense officials, January 2021 and March 2021; and Frank Kenlon, "IA&E in the Adaptive Acquisition Framework (AAF)," Defense Acquisition University, November 12, 2020.

[41] See Australian National Audit Office, *'Wedgetail' Airborne Early Warning and Control Aircraft: Project Management*, Canberra, Australia, 2004, p. 33; "Australia's Troubled E-7A 'Wedgetail' AWACS Program," *Defense Industry Daily*, May 3, 2021; and Australian National Audit Office, *2014–2015 Major Projects Report*, Canberra, Australia, 2016, pp. 195–205, Project Data Summary Sheet for AIR 5077 Phase 3: Airborne Early Warning and Control Aircraft (Wedgetail).

This fact has several unusual effects on U.S.-allied collaboration, including the absence of a U.S. program office to help shepherd the program through internal processes.[42] However, the E-7 appears to be under active consideration by the DAF as a replacement for the aging E-3 Sentry Airborne Warning and Control System, a development that also affects cooperation on the system and the allied ability to conduct force planning.[43] The E-7 Wedgetail case involves several SC activities with the closest and most trusted U.S. allies, including RDT&E, cooperative production, direct commercial sales and Foreign Military Sales, and information-sharing.

Barriers

We identified several barriers to collaboration in this case, including bureaucratic, regulatory, cultural, budgetary, and technical—with constraints on information-sharing underpinning many of these barriers. The most problematic barriers have been bureaucratic and regulatory. U.S. bureaucratic processes associated with foreign disclosure and technology transfer increased the time needed to start collaboration to enhance radar technology.[44] Advances in that technology have increased U.S. sensitivity to technology transfer to Australia even though that ally helped develop the technology for the E-7.[45] The tendency to default to NOFORN on information supporting the E-7 program has further hindered collaboration with Australia and the UK.[46] Regulatory restrictions associated with ITAR have discouraged Australia from sharing innovations for fear of "polluting" and losing access to its own technology if it is incorporated into the E-7.[47] Despite these challenges, the U.S.-allied collaboration has produced a highly capable, malleable platform that highlights iterative, nontraditional collaboration with partners that could become more common with next-generation platforms.

---

[42] Interview with U.S. defense expert, May 2021.

[43] Valerie Insinna, "Top U.S. Air Force General Isn't Ready to Buy E-7 Wedgetail Just Yet," *Defense News*, February 26, 2021.

[44] Foreign disclosure processes allow the U.S. government to factor a variety of considerations, such as national security, economic security, human rights, nonproliferation, and relationships with allies and partners, into its decisions about whether to release information or material to a foreign government. Although many interviewees commented on the barriers associated with foreign disclosure processes, a detailed analysis of the associated steps and timelines was outside of this project's scope. See also U.S. Government Accountability Office, "Conventional Arms Transfer Policy: Agency Processes for Reviewing Direct Commercial Sales and Foreign Military Sales Align with Policy Criteria," Washington, D.C., September 9, 2019, p. 7.

[45] Interviews with foreign defense expert, March 2021; U.S. defense official, April 2021; and U.S. defense expert, May 2021.

[46] Interviews with Australian defense officials, February–May 2021.

[47] Interview with Australian defense official, May 2021.

Defense Technology and Trade Initiative: Air-Launched Unmanned Aerial Vehicle

Background

India and the United States signed an air-launched UAV cooperative development project agreement (PA)[48] in July 2021.[49] The collaboration is the DAF's first cooperative development project with India. It would enable the United States and India to work together to design, build, test, and evaluate a prototype air-launched UAV that could be launched from a cargo aircraft.[50]

For this case study, we looked at the processes used to establish the air-launched UAV PA in the context of the U.S.-India Defense Technology and Trade Initiative (DTTI). The case received senior leader attention in 2019 as a potentially successful DTTI effort.[51] This PA was an activity of the DTTI Air Systems Joint Working Group. Project stakeholders include the U.S. Air Force Research Laboratory and India's Defence Research and Development Organisation's Aeronautical Development Establishment.[52] The Indian Air Force is also a stakeholder, which is unique for PAs between the DAF and India.[53] Although it remains uncertain whether this program will create a successful prototype, the signing of the agreement was considered a major accomplishment, which augured well for future bilateral collaboration.

Barriers

We identified a variety of bureaucratic, budgetary, strategic, cultural, political, regulatory, and technical barriers in the air-launched UAV case with India, in part because of a lack of historical and institutional ties. The continued engagement of high-level champions through the DTTI was instrumental in overcoming bureaucratic obstacles and enabling continued PA development. However, the need to keep leadership informed added to the effort required to establish the PA. Additionally, U.S. fiscal year funding restrictions required U.S. proponents for the PA to identify alternative funds in case it was not signed before the original funding expired.[54] Through fortuitous (or skillful) project selection, the air-launched UAV project was able to avoid many of the barriers, such as U.S. export and equitability requirements, that typically hamper projects between the United States and India. The case also pointed to the

---

[48] A *project agreement* is an international agreement that specifies partner responsibilities and roles for a cooperative effort.

[49] U.S. Air Force, "India and US sign Project Agreement for Air-Launched Unmanned Aerial Vehicle," press release, Arlington, Va., September 3, 2021.

[50] Aaron Mehta, "US, India collaborating on Air-Launched Drone," *Defense News*, March 18, 2019; and Daryl Mayer, "India, US Sign Air-Launched UAV Co-Development Project Agreement," U.S. Air Force, September 3, 2021.

[51] Mehta, 2019.

[52] Mayer, 2021; U.S. Air Force, 2021.

[53] Mayer, 2021; U.S. Air Force, 2021.

[54] Interview with U.S. defense official, March 2021.

importance of strengthening the relationship between the U.S. and Indian air forces: for instance, by incorporating their operational requirements for the UAV.

F-35 Co-Production

Background

This case study addressed Italian participation in the F-35 program, with a particular focus on co-production and interactions among DoD (U.S. Air Force), the U.S. defense industry (Lockheed Martin), Italy's Ministry of Defense (Air Force, Navy, and National Armaments Directorate), and Italian defense industry partners. Italian officials have consistently sought to secure industrial production deals and technology transfers that they viewed as commensurate to their investment (a concept referred to as *just return*),[55] whereas U.S. officials followed a "best value for money" philosophy.[56] Unmet Italian political expectations, as well as divergences in political and military priorities, fueled barriers to co-development.[57] Italian political debates surrounding the F-35 program appeared to briefly threaten Italian participation in the program, though the co-development ultimately succeeded.[58]

This case is relevant for future co-development programs, particularly in the context of the 2022 National Defense Strategy, because the program required the United States to manage a complicated multilateral program. Ultimately, the United States and Italy fulfilled the fundamental parts of the agreement, and interviewees agreed that Italy would likely be willing to conduct future co-production with the United States. Italian frustrations underscored the importance of considering individual partners' political expectations and of ensuring that adequate senior-level attention is devoted to understanding the attitudes and positions of U.S. allies.

Barriers

Although political barriers were the most prominent in this case study, they shaped other barriers as well. There was consensus within the Italian Air Force about the strategic value of the F-35 program, but pacifist elements of the Italian Parliament questioned the program on strategic grounds. Italian expectations regarding defense industrial production deals and technology transfers, which had been important in winning domestic political support for the program, were ultimately unmet and created further tensions, with parliamentary leadership at one point suggesting withdrawal from the program. Bureaucratically, Italian interlocutors felt that a greater degree of attention from senior U.S. defense officials could have mitigated the political

---

[55] Interview with foreign defense expert, March 2021.

[56] Interview with foreign defense expert, March 2021.

[57] Interview with foreign defense expert, March 2021.

[58] Bill Carey, "Italy Begins F-35 Assembly; Dutch Store Their First Two Jets," AINonline, July 26, 2013.

turbulence. Overall, cooperation has largely succeeded despite the hurdles because of the strong bilateral strategic relationship between the United States and Italy and the mutual efforts of U.S. and Italian defense officials to maintain momentum amid domestic political concerns. The establishment of a Final Assembly and Check Out and Maintenance Repair Overhaul and Upgrade facility in Cameri, Italy, helped mitigate some of these concerns. Italian participation in the F-35 program and the establishment of a robust support facility in Italy for allied F-35 operations helped to substantially strengthen combat airpower and interoperability within the North Atlantic Treaty Organization (NATO) alliance.[59]

Combined Security Cooperation Partnering

Background

Although this case originally was cross-domain focused, we could only find evidence of some limited activity in the air domain. There is an irregular SC practice of partnering with an ally to conduct SC together in a third country. Although we reached out to various air component commands, we did not find evidence of a global, concerted effort to work with allies in SC in third countries. In Europe, perhaps this is because the UK, France, Sweden, and other NATO allies compete with the United States in military sales and may not see a clear advantage of working together in third countries. We found some limited evidence of combined SC partnering in the U.S. Indo-Pacific Command area of responsibility.[60] U.S. Indo-Pacific Command's Multinational Working Group is unique in its focus on helping identify opportunities to work with allies in third countries. The Multinational Working Group includes members from the FVEY countries, plus Japan and France.[61] We found that the DAF is involved in the planning and execution of activities at the component level, but most of the drive and the design comes from the U.S. embassy in-country teams, who can coordinate directly with the allied in-country teams. There is little evidence of a DAF headquarters (SAF/IA or Headquarters, Department of the Air Force [HAF] A-5/8) role.

Barriers

There is much work to be done in combined SC partnering. We found that, in practice, DoD SC planners tend to focus on deconflicting to identify overlaps and gaps and sometimes focus on coordinating engagements. An example of deconfliction would be for the United States, Japan, and Australia to compare plans for engaging with a nation in Oceania and then identify gaps or overlapping activities. Coordination in combined SC partnering is a bit more involved: Working

---

[59] Robbin Laird, "Lessons Learned at Cameri, Italy's F-35 HQ: Implications for Asia," *Breaking Defense*, November 4, 2013.

[60] Interviews with U.S. defense officials, March and May 2021.

[61] See Jennifer D. P. Moroney and Alan Tidwell, "America's Strategy in Oceania: Time for a Better Approach," *War on the Rocks*, July 19, 2021.

in country X, the United States trains the pilots, Japan trains the maintainers, and Australia focuses on precursory English-language training for both. But we found little evidence to support the regular practice of combined SC planning with key U.S. allies outside of warzones, such as Afghanistan. We observed several barriers in the SC partnering case study, including political, strategic, bureaucratic, budgetary, and cultural barriers.

Air Domain–Specific Barriers

In this section, we identify barriers we found that are specific to the air domain. Given our limited number of case studies, we cannot be certain that these barriers do not appear elsewhere in the space or cyber domains.

In the air domain, we found that **differences in strategic priorities (with the United States seeking to create new capabilities while its partner wishes to obtain U.S. technology) can lead to unrealized expectations and diminished cooperation**. For cooperative development particularly, there can be discrepancies with SC objectives, potentially creating political barriers. In the F-35 case, the United States sought to create new capabilities while Italy sought to obtain U.S. technology and strengthen its defense industry.

Potential mitigation strategies include the following:

- increase service-level engagement to focus on common operational needs
- increase bilateral defense exchanges in RDT&E and cooperative development to improve coordination and understanding of expectations, capabilities, and needs
- clarify expectations regarding approaches, priorities, and government and industry roles early in collaborative programs.

The relevant stakeholder communities are foreign disclosure, operations, policy, and SC planning.

Space Domain Cases

Wideband Global SATCOM

Background

WGS provides wideband, high-data-rate communications to the U.S. military, the White House, the U.S. Department of State, and international partners that have signed cooperative agreements.[62] The first WGS satellite launched in 2007; the most recent satellite, WGS-10, began orbiting in November 2019.[63] We selected this case because it had classification and cost-sharing challenges associated with an expanding pool of international participants.

---

[62] U.S. Air Force, "Wideband Global SATCOM Satellite," webpage, November 23, 2015.

[63] Congress appropriated funds for two additional satellites in 2018. DoD plans to fulfill the intent behind these funds by launching a single satellite with twice the capacity, referred to as *WGS-11+* (Department of Defense,

The WGS program began as a stopgap between the legacy Defense Satellite Communications System and an intended follow-on program, the Transformational Satellite Communications System (TSAT). When TSAT was canceled, the U.S. Air Force purchased additional WGS satellites, making WGS the DoD's primary military satellite communications (MILSATCOM) program.[64] The initial design of WGS satellites appeared to be similar to existing commercial satellites, conveying an expectation of minimal RDT&E and thus lower cost.[65] WGS costs, however, unexpectedly increased.[66] International partnerships presented the opportunity to ease the increasing cost burden while maintaining the program's tempo. Partners were to fund the procurement of satellites in exchange for proportionate access to the constellation's bandwidth, although the U.S.-Australian cooperation went further, given Australia's contribution of cooperative project personnel for operational planning.[67]

Barriers

The WGS program encountered budgetary, bureaucratic, cultural, political, regulatory, and technical barriers, varying by the negotiation, implementation, and operations stages. Although strategic alignment and senior leader engagement facilitated workarounds and mitigations, the budgetary, bureaucratic, and technical barriers remained the most problematic. U.S. bureaucratic processes associated with foreign disclosure and technology transfer added to the time needed to start collaboration and resulted in missed opportunities for allies. The large size of the U.S. bureaucracy—and the lack of a single, defined point of contact for collaboration—created challenges for partners with smaller staffs. An inability to share timely information also resulted in missed acquisitions and operations opportunities for partners. WGS is widely recognized as a successful cooperative effort but only because of significant efforts to find workarounds for the barriers to cooperation.

Selected Acquisition Report: Wideband Global SATCOM (WGS) as of FY2020 President's Budget, Washington, D.C., December 2018c).

[64] Yool Kim, Elliot Axelband, Abby Doll, Mel Eisman, Myron Hura, Edward G. Keating, Martin C. Libicki, Bradley Martin, Michael E. McMahon, Jerry M. Sollinger, Erin York, Mark V. Arena, Irv Blickstein, and William Shelton, *Acquisition of Space Systems, Volume 7: Past Problems and Future Challenges*, Santa Monica, Calif.: RAND Corporation, MG-1171/7-OSD, 2015, pp. 19–22.

[65] Kim et al., 2015, pp. 19–22.

[66] Kim et al., 2015, pp. 19–22.

[67] U.S. Department of Defense and Australian Department of Defence, Memorandum of Understanding Between the Department of Defense of the United States of America and the Department of Defence of Australia Concerning Joint Production, Operations, and Support of Wideband Global Satellite Communications, Washington, D.C., November 14, 2007; and Canadian Department of National Defence, Danish Ministry of Defence, Luxembourgish Minister of Defence, Dutch Minister of Defence, New Zealand Defence Force, and U.S. Department of Defence, Memorandum of Understanding Among the Department of National Defence of Canada and the Ministry of Defence of the Kingdom of Denmark and the Minister of Defence of the Grand Duchy of Luxembourg and the Minister of Defence of the Kingdom of the Netherlands and the New Zealand Defence Force and the Department of Defense of the United States of America Concerning the Joint Production, Operations, and Support of Wideband Global Satellite Communications, 2012, as amended in 2017 with the addition of the Danish Ministry of Defence.

Arctic Military Satellite Communications System

Background

We selected this case because it represents a first-of-its-kind DoD payload arrangement (U.S. payload on an allied nation's satellite, procured from and launched by U.S. industry) that could shape future space SC.

The Arctic MILSATCOM system is a joint production initiative between Norway and the United States. The initiative centers on the United States deploying payloads on two Norwegian-procured satellites, starting in 2023.[68] It originated with a DoD examination in the mid-2010s of options for hosting the Enhanced Polar System-Recapitalization payload.[69] At approximately the same time, Norway sought partners to share costs on an Arctic Satellite Broadband Mission project to provide new broadband capability for military and nonmilitary users in the region.

Barriers

The Arctic Satellite Broadband Mission effort experienced budgetary, bureaucratic, regulatory, cultural, and technical barriers, with bureaucratic and regulatory barriers being the most problematic. As with the WGS case, the complex U.S. system seemed overly bureaucratic to allies and resulted in a Memorandum of Understanding (MOU) negotiation process that took almost two years. Even this timeline was faster than normal, thanks to senior leader engagement that kept the pressure on minimally staffed U.S. space cooperation organizations. U.S. regulatory barriers related to acquisition models and risk postures were also problematic for the Arctic Satellite Broadband Mission. The United States and Norway were able to overcome the barriers because of creative workarounds, such as the use of an undefinitized contract action and compromise on validation and verification testing details. Although the Arctic MILSATCOM system faced challenges throughout the partnership, both parties demonstrated flexibility and determination to implement mitigations, demonstrating how leadership and creativity are critical to SC with highly capable allies.

Quasi-Zenith Satellite System

Background

The final space case study examines the cooperative effort between the United States and Japan to host U.S. payloads on Japan's QZSS. The initiative centers on the United States deploying space domain awareness payloads on two Japanese satellites, starting in 2023.[70] The

---

[68] U.S. Air Force and Norwegian Ministry of Defence, Artic Satellite Communications Memorandum of Agreement, May 28, 2019.

[69] Interview with civilian subject-matter expert, March 2021.

[70] U.S. Department of State, "Joint Statement on the Sixth Meeting of the U.S.-Japan Comprehensive Dialogue on Space," July 24, 2019.

26

partnership represents the first foreign government–hosted payload on a satellite procured and launched through the ally's industry.

Japan launched its first QZSS demonstrator in 2010 and has continued efforts to develop seven satellites by 2023.[71] Although the United States and Japan discussed various options for increased space SC over the years, it was not until 2019 that both countries publicly stated they were planning the QZSS payload.[72] Although the National Aeronautics and Space Administration (NASA) and the Japan Aerospace Exploration Agency have a long history of cooperating on civilian space projects, cooperation between the U.S. military and the office responsible for QZSS was new. This case is also interesting because the U.S. payload plan changed over the course of the discussions and during the COVID-19 pandemic.

Barriers

QZSS experienced strategic, bureaucratic, regulatory, technical, and cultural barriers, with strategic and bureaucratic barriers being the most problematic. The lack of a common rationale for cooperation not only slowed progress but also led to a major payload change, which became necessary when Japan would not allow the United States to exceed payload weight restrictions or delay the launch schedule. The result was a space domain awareness capability that the United States arguably did not need but pursued for the overall sake of cooperation. This was a reasonable decision, given the significant bureaucratic barriers faced throughout the process, ranging from an inadequate understanding of each nation's system to security challenges. With this significant change, the QZSS effort is on track at the time of this writing and is an important step toward future space partnerships between the United States and Japan, because it provides a framework for future collaboration in space domain awareness, SATCOM, and (potentially) counter-space and missile warning.

Space Domain–Specific Barriers

In addition to our cross-domain findings, we found that **the large size and complexity of these programs, as well as the lack of a single voice across the U.S. space SC enterprise, challenge the scale and pace of collaboration**. This barrier was apparent in all three case studies.

In the WGS case, the U.S. system complexity was apparent throughout both the negotiation and implementation stages. For example, DoD has over 100 terminal programs across the services: If an ally is to acquire U.S.-made terminals, it must navigate this milieu one program at a time. A joint terminal program office, or at least a mechanism to help guide interested allies and partners, does not exist.

---

[71] Interview with Japanese space subject-matter expert, March 2021.

[72] U.S. Department of State, 2019.

In the case of the Arctic MILSATCOM program, Norwegian familiarity with the U.S. SC process and willingness to adopt the U.S. government template for Memoranda of Agreement (MOAs) helped streamline a bureaucratic process that nonetheless continuously hampered progress.

In the QZSS case, delays were caused by Japan, which wanted to use similar language from a previous U.S.-Japan MOU awaiting final approval. Delays were further exacerbated because Japan also did not understand why the United States later wanted "tweaks" to the agreement after negotiations had completed and approval was received, requiring U.S. partners to explain that different stakeholders came to the discussion at different times with different edits. The QZSS case was noteworthy because there was a public announcement in 2019 that an MOU was imminent but then there was a yearlong delay over specific legal terms.

Potential mitigation strategies include the following:

- ensure timely senior leader (within and outside the DAF) attention, with the understanding that this is a scarce resource, on issues for which there is internal U.S. government disagreement (e.g., security-related risk tolerance) to reduce the friction from the complex U.S. system; for example, DAF leadership could initiate a review of all programs in which highly capable allies and partners are involved to ensure there is (1) a single-office point of contact and (2) a communication strategy for the more complex and more sensitive programs for which allies and partners do not have full access
- provide a single coordinating authority to lead negotiations and facilitate dialogue across U.S. stakeholders
- centralize functions where practical (e.g., create a joint terminal program for operations or a single point of contact for partners for space SC).

The relevant stakeholder communities are operations, policy and SC planning, and weapons and acquisition.

Another important barrier in the space domain is that **DAF and other U.S. organizations have limited human resources to enable the level of space SC envisioned by strategy**. It is common for action officers and staffs in all domains to claim there are insufficient resources to accomplish the mission. For space, the significant emphasis on international space cooperation and consistent comments from a wide variety of staffs demonstrates that this challenge is more than just rhetoric. There are specific examples of this observation in the WGS and QZSS case studies. There has been recent emphasis within the U.S. Space Force to place greater priority on international space cooperation, but it is not yet clear if a potential reorganization will result in more human capital. In addition, Foreign Military Sales has built-in fees to cover costs for such items as staff work to formulate and negotiate agreements, but this is not the case for international armaments cooperation. The space SC enterprise has been able to push through a few key cooperative cases with limited resources, largely because of significant efforts from the staffs. For example, we were told that the Office of the Under Secretary of Defense for Acquisition and Sustainment has one government and two contractor personnel available to review all international agreements.[73] Also, SAF/IA for space has a much smaller number of personnel than the air domain, yet the growing emphasis on space SC seems likely to result in more demand for space professionals on the staff. Failure to rightsize this staff could result in fewer SC agreements or fewer agreements at the brisk pace envisioned by strategy.

A potential mitigation strategy is that DAF should conduct a strategy-to-task analysis to better understand the extent of personnel shortfalls for expanding SC with allies and partners. The relevant stakeholder communities are manpower and training and policy and SC planning.

Overall, we recommend that the International Space Cooperation Enterprise Working Group review our case studies and mitigation strategies in its efforts to resolve impediments to space SC.

Cyber Domain Cases

Cyber domain cases differ slightly from the air and space domain. Cyber relations tend to be relatively nascent; they also tend to only exist with highly capable allies and partners. For this reason, the United States and its allies and partners are still very much in the process of establishing collaborations rather than developing large, ambitious co-development programs. Hence, the cyber domain cases we examine—U.S.-Australia, U.S.-Estonia, and U.S.-Finland—focus on relationships rather than, as in the air and space domains, specific programs.

U.S.-Australia

Background

Cyber cooperation between the United States and Australia has existed since World War II but has matured significantly since 2009, especially since U.S. and Australian operational cyber support to the U.S. Central Command–led Combined Joint Task Force – Operation Inherent Resolve in 2016.[74] U.S.-Australian military cyber collaboration has grown from computer network defense activities to include cooperation across a full range of cyberspace activities. In 2018, DoD and the Australian Department of Defence signed an RDT&E MOU to enable cyber capability development. Since then, multiple PAs supporting cyber capability development initiatives have been developed under the umbrella RDT&E agreement.[75]

The U.S.-Australia cyber partnership is an interesting case study because of Australia's status as a FVEY partner, the historic signals intelligence (SIGINT) partnership between the two nations, and Australian experience with integrating cyber effects into past and current named

---

[73] Interview with civilian subject-matter expert, March 2021.

[74] Mark Pomerleau, "How Cyber Command Can Limit the Reach of ISIS," *C4ISRNET*, September 17, 2019. See also Stephanie Borys, "Licence to Hack: Using a Keyboard to Fight Islamic State," *ABC News Australia*, December 17, 2019.

[75] U.S. Cyber Command, "US and Australia Sign First-Ever Cyber Agreement to Develop Virtual Training Range," press release, Fort George G. Meade, Md., December 4, 2020.

operations. It is also interesting because of the bureaucratic and regulatory structures that support cyber effects-based collaboration between military and SIGINT organizations, which U.S. laws, policies, and structures intentionally keep stovepiped.[76] Finally, the barriers and challenges of this collaboration provide an informative contrast to those in other, non-FVEY case studies. Many of the challenges and barriers in this relationship are also evident in other cyber case studies, suggesting that even Australia's status as one of the closest and most advanced U.S. allies is insufficient to overcome some barriers that limit collaboration.

Barriers

We identified four main barriers—strategic, bureaucratic, regulatory, and technical—to cyber collaboration with Australia, with constraints relating to timely information-sharing in a constantly evolving environment being common across each of these barriers and strategic and regulatory barriers being the most problematic and mutually reinforcing. At the strategic level, U.S. and Australian cyber leadership have acknowledged the need to operate together at the speed of cyber, but we identified numerous obstacles that have prevented this. These include challenges related to information-sharing and technical capability development, as well as legal or regulatory challenges. Although Australia is a FVEY and SIGINT partner, the time needed to execute the foreign disclosure process and the U.S. tendency to "default to NOFORN" (i.e., not writing for release) have contributed to problems with sharing timely information. Furthermore, the lack of technical solutions to enable the sharing of cyber intelligence in support of command and control, planning, targeting, and execution limits allies' ability to quickly respond to emerging threats or threats in evolving multidomain environments. Finally, the regulatory barriers relating to the foreign disclosure process and reliance on international armaments cooperation to enable combined action in cyberspace limit the degree to which the United States and Australia can respond to new incidents, especially those that may occur on nonmilitary critical infrastructure.

U.S.-Estonia

Background

The second cyber domain case study examines the partnership between the United States and Estonia. We examine this partnership for several reasons. First, given Estonia's geographical location, strategic disposition, and status as a highly capable ally in cyberspace, the advancement

---

[76] Although U.S. SIGINT organizations (primarily, the National Security Agency) support the development of Title 10 military cyber effects (or offensive cyber operations) by providing relevant SIGINT under their Title 50 intelligence authorities, the delineation of Title 10 (military) and Title 50 (intelligence) authorities creates clear boundaries that determine the specific activities that can be conducted under Title 10 and Title 50 authorities in cyberspace. Unlike the United States, Australia's intelligence and cyber operations laws do not restrict or limit the ability of Australia's SIGINT organization (the Australian Signals Directorate) from supporting, enabling, and executing the full spectrum of cyberspace operations. This agile regulatory and organizational structure provides an interesting comparison to the U.S. legal and organizational model regarding actions taken in cyberspace.

of the cyber partnership is a high U.S. priority. Second, despite the value of the partnership, the structures and processes for developing cooperation with Estonia are limited because Estonia does not benefit from an established SIGINT partnership. Third, both the United States and Estonia desire and have opportunities for greater cyber collaboration, particularly in such areas as cybersecurity, but have not been able to realize them because of U.S. bureaucratic limitations and resource challenges.[77] For example, the relevant U.S. agency for engagement on cybersecurity is the Cybersecurity and Infrastructure Security Agency at the Department of Homeland Security, but this agency is limited to partnering with a few countries and has limited manpower and resources for engaging Estonia.[78]

Cyber collaboration between the two countries began in 2008 and has matured significantly. Estonia has greater cyber maturity than other similar nations. It desires collaboration across the full spectrum of cyberspace activities and can lead regional cybersecurity capacity-building. Priorities for the partnership include shared cyber situational awareness, collaboration on and support to full-spectrum cyber operations, cyber exercises and training, cyber capability and infrastructure development, and cybersecurity policy and implementation.

To achieve these shared objectives, the U.S. and Estonia conduct international armaments cooperation under a 2016 RDT&E MOU, an annual slate of cyber exercises, and regular cyber threat and cyber information-sharing,[79] with the partnership involving numerous DoD and interagency stakeholders.[80]

Barriers

The U.S.-Estonia partnership confronts five categories of barriers: strategic, bureaucratic, regulatory, budgetary, and technical. The most problematic barriers in this relationship are technical and bureaucratic. A key technical barrier is the lack of platforms to share electronic classified information. The United States uses the Battlefield Information Collection and Exploitation System (BICES) to share classified information with the Estonian Ministry of Defense, but this system is inaccessible to other Estonian government entities, such as the Ministry Foreign Affairs and Estonian Information System Authority. This hampers allies' ability to attribute malicious cyber activity or mount a coordinated, timely response to a cyberattack. It also poses security concerns because of the need to "talk around" the problem on unclassified systems. A key bureaucratic barrier to collaboration is the rigid U.S. delineation of cyber organizations, funding, and authorities. Estonia takes a more holistic approach to these issues and, as a result, has a variety of public and private parties involved in its cybersecurity mission. The number of agencies involved makes strictly military-to-military collaboration

---

[77] Interview with U.S. officials, April 2021.

[78] Interview with U.S. officials, April 2021.

[79] DoD, "U.S., Estonia Sign Defense Research Agreement," June 22, 2016.

[80] Interviews with U.S. officials, January and April 2021.

difficult and often does not address Estonia's priorities. For example, one of Estonia's priorities is building its whole-of-society cybersecurity capabilities in partnership with the United States. However, the funding and mechanisms to do so on the U.S. side are somewhat constrained, because the relevant U.S. agency for cybersecurity engagement has limited manpower, resources, and authorities to engage with international partners.

One strategic barrier in the U.S.-Estonia cyber partnership has been mitigated. Officials interviewed for this study noted that, in earlier phases of the partnership, a significant barrier to effective cooperation was the large number of U.S. actors involved. This impeded cohesive, unified, and synchronized cyber cooperation between the allies. However, this strategic planning barrier has largely been mitigated through the joint development of a framework that establishes specific goals and tasks and tracks progress among U.S. and Estonian cyber actors.

U.S.-Finland

Background

The third cyber case study examines the U.S. cyber partnership with Finland. In 2016, DoD signed a bilateral defense Statement of Intent with Finland's Ministry of Defense to promote security in the Baltic Sea region, strengthen stability in northern Europe, and build interoperability between U.S. and Finnish forces.[81] The Statement of Intent served as the strategic guidance under which the U.S. Air Force negotiated and, in December 2020, signed a master Information Exchange Agreement with Finland on the research and development of cyber technologies. The U.S. Air Force is also developing an Engineer and Scientist Exchange Program agreement with Finland to support collaboration on cyber and cyber-related technologies.[82]

Since 2016, numerous departments and agencies across the Finnish Ministry of Defense have experienced substantial growth in their workforce: specifically, to support current and emerging cyber requirements. Finland has also developed cybersecurity centers and other, similar entities. Cyber is a priority for the Finnish military, as reflected in the growing cyber research and development tasks and requirements placed on the Finnish Defense Research Agency. The Finnish Air Force has also prioritized enhancing command, control, computers, communications, cyber, intelligence, surveillance, and reconnaissance and general cyber situational awareness,

---

[81] U.S. Department of Defense and Finnish Ministry of Defense, Statement of Intent Between the Department of Defense of the United States and the Ministry of Defense of the Republic of Finland, Helsinki, October 7, 2016.

[82] Interviews with U.S. defense officials, March and April 2021.

including in collaboration with the U.S. Air Force.[83] Finland works closely with the other five Nordic countries on several cooperative defense activities, including cyber.[84]

Finland, which is neither a FVEY country nor a NATO member, provides an interesting contrast with the other case studies. Its support for strategic deterrence initiatives, geographic location, reputation as a technologically advanced and cyber-resilient nation, and prioritization within the U.S. cyber community also contributed to its inclusion in this report.

Barriers

We identified several barriers to U.S.-Finland collaboration (particularly, strategic, bureaucratic, regulatory, and technical challenges), with information-sharing constraints contributing to each of the barriers and with bureaucratic and regulatory barriers being the most problematic. As in the other case studies, the bureaucratic and regulatory processes governing foreign disclosure and information sharing, particularly of information the United States has marked NOFORN, have created challenges in sharing relevant theater campaign plans and supporting planning materials. Regulatory and bureaucratic challenges related to information-sharing limit areas for collaboration and capability development and may even contribute to duplication of effort. Additionally, the bureaucratic misalignment of relevant cyber organizations, as well as these organizations' differing legal mandates, limits strictly military-to-military collaboration in cyberspace. Like Estonia, Finland approaches cybersecurity and cyber defense from a holistic perspective. The number of nonmilitary cyber organizations involved in these issues makes military-to-military collaboration challenging. Interestingly, Finnish organizations responsible for cyber intelligence and effects operations align better with U.S. cyber entities with similar responsibilities and may make collaboration on offensive cyber easier than coordination on defensive cyber. Finally, Finland's domestic transparency laws relating to defense spending and defense activities present regulatory challenges that complicate the U.S.-Finland cyber partnership. All Finnish defense activities and spending require the approval of Finland's parliamentarians—which makes such initiatives subject to public opinion. As a result, Finnish defense and cyber officials may be unwilling to discuss cyber collaboration or capability development activities unless they are certain of public support for them.

Cyber Domain–Specific Barriers

In the cyber domain, the most notable barrier is that **the United States and its allies and partners often have differing views over what they consider to be "sensitive" information**. This issue arose in the case of cyber cooperation with Finland, which has strict domestic

---

[83] Interview with foreign defense official, February 2021.

[84] Sean Cordey, "Finland," in Robert S. Dewar, ed., *National Cybersecurity and Cyberdefense Policy Snapshots*, Zürich, Switzerland: Center for Security Studies, September 2018, p. 36; and Danish Ministry of Defence, *NORDEFCO Annual Report 2020*, Copenhagen, 2020.

transparency laws requiring the intelligence and defense communities to report activities to the Parliament of Finland and the public. As a result, information relating to national defense activities, including in cyberspace, is highly stovepiped and limited to secure or in-person communication. The COVID-19 pandemic and resulting travel restrictions magnified this challenge and highlighted the degree to which robust cyber collaboration between the United States and Finland is hampered by the lack of secure and classified collaborative infrastructure.

Potential mitigation strategies include the following:

- develop secure collaborative infrastructure between the United States and partner cyber organizations to discuss issues that are unclassified for the United States but classified for partners
- increase the information security community's role in working with allies and partners to (1) develop a shared understanding of what is sensitive and (2) establish security controls that protect the information in a way that meets cyber community operational needs and addresses U.S. intelligence concerns.

The relevant stakeholder communities are information security and policy and SC planning.

Another important barrier observed in our cyber case studies is **the lack of advocacy for, and clear prioritization of, the agreements that the United States should be pursuing and the types of technology it should be developing with allies and partners**. For example, cyber technical experts, cyber operators at the combatant commands, and cyber enablers within the acquisition and strategic planning communities emphasized that the guidance they used to prioritize cyber capability development was often too broad or too detailed and was not well connected to operational requirements. We also noted a lack of senior leader advocacy for the development of specific technologies and, relatedly, the prioritization of international agreements to enable combined capability development. This barrier, which we found in each cyber case study, results in insufficient guidance for those implementing SC agreements and stretches their limited resources. In some cases, agreements have been left dormant because of a lack of advocacy or prioritization by the requesting organization and limited personnel responsible for staffing agreements.

Potential mitigation strategies include the following:

- ensure cyber senior leadership advocates for critical technologies with priority partners to technical experts and research labs to identify priorities
- ensure cyber and research leadership vocalize the prioritization and urgency of specific agreements to the foreign disclosure and agreements community.

The relevant stakeholder communities are foreign disclosure and policy and SC planning.

Conclusion

Our case studies focused on more-complex or more-novel programs. This approach may distort our findings, particularly relative to excluded cases that did not receive substantial DAF involvement. Nevertheless, these barriers could become more prevalent as the United States develops new programs and new ways to increase cooperation with its most capable allies and partners. Table 3.2 summarizes the mitigation strategies we identified for these barriers and the case studies to which these strategies may be most relevant.

Table 3.2. Domain-Specific Barriers and Related Case Studies

Barriers	Related Case Studies
Air Domain	
Differences in strategic priorities (for instance, when the United States is seeking to create new capabilities while its partner wishes to obtain U.S. technology) can lead to unrealized expectations and diminished cooperation.	• Defense Technology and Trade Initiative: Air-Launched UAV • F-35 Co-Production • Combined SC Partnering
Space Domain	
The large size and complexity of these programs and the lack of a single voice across the U.S. space SC enterprise challenge the scale and pace of collaboration.	• WGS • Arctic MILSATCOM System • QZSS
DAF and other U.S. organizations have limited human resources to enable the level of space SC envisioned by strategy.	• WGS • QZSS
Cyber Domain	
The United States and its allies and partners often have differing views over what they consider to be sensitive information.	• U.S.-Finland
There is a lack of advocacy for, and clear prioritization of, the agreements that the United States should be pursuing and the types of technology it should be developing with allies and partners.	• U.S.-Australia • U.S.-Estonia • U.S.-Finland

Although this chapter focused on barriers we identified within a single domain according to the cases we selected, many were evident in cases across domains. In the next chapter, we review these cross-domain barriers, as well as mitigation strategies for each and the stakeholders that might implement these strategies.

Chapter 4. Cross-Domain Observations and Mitigation Strategies

Our case studies identified seven *cross-domain barriers*: that is, barriers that we observed in two or more domains. These are

- allies and partners rarely included in concept and system development phases
- limited extent and speed of communication
- lack of technical collaborative infrastructure
- slow bureaucratic execution
- U.S. regulations impeding rather than supporting SC
- failure to account for political constraint of allies and partners
- lack of incentive, tasking, and understanding of priorities for combined partnering in third countries.

We discuss these barriers further in this chapter, as well as potential mitigation strategies and the relevant stakeholders for implementation.

Cross-Domain Barrier 1: Allies and Partners Are Rarely Included in Concept and System Development Phases

Across all three domains, we found that the lack of involvement of allies and partners in the earliest phases of a program—specifically, the concept and system development phases—could result in misunderstandings, delays, and, ultimately, suboptimal outcomes. In the QZSS case, a lack of early coordination on specific mission objectives and timelines led to the need to change the payload, showing how major changes to the purpose or design of an acquisition posed lengthy delays in cooperation. In the Australia cyber case, a lack of early coordination on the Persistent Cyber Training Environment led to misunderstandings on the level and type of collaborative development needed for development of the capability.

Although there is guidance on incorporating allies and partners in the acquisition process, it is implemented inconsistently. To be fair, we note that such early involvement of allies and partners can be challenging. In the ABMS case, challenges included the changing scope of the program, broad organizational participation, imperatives of rapid acquisition, and information-sharing constraints. Such involvement also cannot be done systematically: In F-35 co-production with Italy, the United States could hardly share more than it did because of the sensitivity of the technology. Hence, how to involve allies or partners must be decided on a case-by-case basis. Still, involving allies and partners early on remains important for projects that directly affect their investments, if only to set realistic expectations for future phases and improvements.

Potential mitigation strategies include the following:

- **Review guidance and policies regarding the incorporation of allies into early concept development and acquisition.** Such guidance exists for major acquisition programs to support international cooperation and the exportability of the system being developed. But there is no equivalent for urgent capability acquisition or for middle-tier acquisition programs, given concerns of possibly overburdening small programs with tight time constraints. For early concept development, some requirement documents mention allies but typically do not include a lot of depth. It would be helpful for guidance about how and when to work with allies and partners to be more specific and more direct.

- **Consider innovative ways to involve allies and partners in key concept development discussions and programs beyond nonreciprocal exchanges.** Involving allies and partners in concept development and early acquisition require time, such as for additional foreign disclosure needs. Planning for accelerated foreign disclosure review of the information to be released could facilitate this involvement. This could be done through a joint Terms of Reference backed on the U.S. side with a Delegated Disclosure Authority Letter that gives a technical lead the authority to share with particular partners within defined constraints—a setup that would require international affairs resources. A related challenge is the difficulty in communicating the uncertainty associated with early program concepts. The United States does not want partners to make major decisions based on preliminary information that is subject to change.

- **Reexamine the potential impact of not sharing advances in technology with the closest allies.** For example, what is the operational effect of not having fully integrated battle management capabilities for the United States and its highly capable allies? Or what opportunities to jointly advance radar capabilities might be dashed because the United States prefers to provide "black boxes" rather than the underlying technology on Wedgetails for Australia and the UK? Senior DAF leaders might ask similar questions about potential opportunity costs when considering the utility of providing allied access to U.S. technology.

The relevant stakeholder communities are concept formulation and development, foreign disclosure, operations, policy and SC planning, and weapons and acquisition.

Cross-Domain Barrier 2: Limited Extent and Speed of Communication

The issue of communication—what needs to be communicated, how often, and to whom—cuts across multiple domains. Lack of communication, or disjointed communication, appear to be particularly problematic, not just leading to misunderstandings and delays but also to potential friction, particularly when U.S. allies and partners learn about program developments through other sources than their U.S. interlocutors.[85] This happened in the ABMS case, in which allies received information from news media on issues that affected their force planning. In the Wedgetail case, DAF indecision and lack of communication created uncertainty for Australian and UK force planning.

---

[85] The case of disjointed communication is also reminiscent of one of the barriers we identified across our space case studies: The large size and complexity of these programs and the lack of a single voice across the U.S. space SC enterprise challenge the scale and pace of collaboration.

This barrier can be both bureaucratic and cultural. This is the case for the default use of NOFORN classification—or any other incorrect or inadequate markings and practices—which creates major impediments to information-sharing and coordination. In the WGS case, one of the causes of the delays was that some documents were marked NOFORN even though they did not need to be, per policy. This required the Foreign Disclosure Office's involvement, affecting mission planning and responsiveness to access requests.[86] This issue also arose in several other cases and shows that, even though there are increasing efforts to avoid using NOFORN (particularly in the space domain), the habit or culture of doing so might take longer to change, particularly because underclassifying by mistake could come at a high professional cost for the personnel involved in these decisions.[87]

Allies and partners that involve government agencies beyond their ministries of defense in SC programs can find themselves particularly at a disadvantage. In the U.S.-Estonia cyber cooperation case, BICES was not accessible to the Estonian Ministry of Foreign Affairs and other Estonian government entities. Similar technological barriers to sharing information with non–Ministry of Defense entities arose in the QZSS case. Although the United States and Japan have agreements for their defense organizations to share classified information, QZSS is not a military satellite, leading to questions on how to share and safeguard classified information or sensitive technology with the Mitsubishi Electric Corporation and the prime minister's office.[88] In some cases, workarounds have been attempted, without success. Indeed, some created more problems than they solved. For instance, the reliance on SIPRNet Releasable (SIPR REL) terminals for Australian embeds, or Foreign Exchange Officers, in the United States did not improve communication challenges or enable operational collaboration. However, because it created a perception that a solution had been found, interviewees reported an apparent hesitance by U.S. leadership to develop a different solution. As a workaround, one U.S. organization created NOFORN exemptions for Australian embedded personnel to ensure they could receive U.S.-only operational planning documents that were necessary to perform their duties. Nevertheless, these exemptions did not yield the intended result and further contributed to a U.S. belief that the barrier had been resolved. This suggests that communities of interest should be consulted on the efficiency of proposed or attempted workarounds. It also suggests the importance of revisiting temporary solutions if they do not fully address a persistent issue.

---

[86] Interview with civilian subject-matter experts, March 2021.

[87] The DAF is in the process of pursuing several initiatives to improve the education of its classifying authorities and streamline the workforce responsible for original classification (interview with U.S. defense official, July 2021). See also Inspector General of the U.S. Department of Defense, *DoD Evaluation of Over-Classification of National Security Information*, Alexandria, Va., September 30, 2013; and Inspector General of the U.S. Department of Defense, *Follow Up to DoD Evaluation of Over-Classification of National Security Information*, Alexandria, Va., December 1, 2016.

[88] Interview with Japanese space subject-matter expert, March 2021. These differences in security protocols mattered because the U.S. National Security Agency is providing encryption in the hosted payload, and the hosted payload itself is secure (U.S. official, roundtable discussion, May 11, 2021).

Potential mitigation strategies include the following:

- **Provide incentive in policy, guidance, and senior-leader statements to encourage the release of information or technology to specific groups or countries.** It is important to make the early resolution of discussions on release a priority and to be ready to escalate disagreements quickly so that senior leadership can resolve them and allow the program to proceed on a predictable schedule with the necessary safeguards. Such incentives might also come from an increased effort to incorporate a risk-benefit analysis that accounts for the operational impact of not sharing information or technology. We understand, however, that such an analysis may add an additional layer to an already complex process and go against the idea of streamlining foreign disclosure processes, described below.

- **Incentivize sharing while disincentivizing defaulting to NOFORN** in the following ways:

  - create justification tabs requiring Division Chief/O-6 or higher approval of anything stamped NOFORN
  - increase the visibility of efforts to streamline the use of NOFORN, including improving training for classification originators and promoting the understanding that NOFORN is not appropriate if the information raises no intelligence issues
  - develop training on how to use Controlled Unclassified Information (CUI) and ensure that CUI is marked appropriately and releasable to partners, when possible
  - publicize the benefits of sharing through foreign disclosure training and information security training more generally (promoting a change of mindset).

- **Streamline communication by ensuring allies and partners are fully aware of the government-to-government channels throughout the process.** In some cases, this will require managing the number of U.S. organizations that interface with the partner. Cyber cooperation cases show that the sheer number of U.S. organizations interfacing with partners make it difficult to formalize, mature, plan, and align activities with strategy. In other cases, this might involve helping the ally or partner streamline communication. The overall purpose is to reduce confusion, eliminate redundancy in communication, and provide faster coordinated answers.

- **During early discussions on a program, agree with the ally or partner on standard operating procedures for the communication of sensitive but unclassified information.** For greater effectiveness, such options could be agreed to above the program level. Ideally, specific standard operating procedures would be adopted with each ally or partner and replicated across programs.

- **Fully leverage personnel exchanges and foreign exchange officers within the RDT&E community, as well as within the operational, acquisition, and domain-specific commands.** Personnel exchange programs provide an opportunity for quicker, enhanced communication with allies and partners. One approach can be to customize personnel exchanges to maximize the information that liaison officers (LNOs) can access and share with their country of origin. Personnel exchanges could also be systematically included in bilateral talks as a standard agenda item or deliverable and could be considered during the MOU development phase. Finally, it might be useful to increase the number of reciprocal exchanges to facilitate two-way information and, for the cyber domain, to increase the presence of U.S. cyber personnel in-country (LNOs, Foreign Exchange Officers, and Military Personnel Exchange Program participants, among others). We recognize that this is a complex issue that could include a need to revisit relevant policies (for instance, asking whether more dual-hatted positions should be allowed) and requires more research.

- **Place designated, domain-specific LNOs at equivalent organizations in ally and partner countries and at relevant Centers of Excellence.** One such organization could be the NATO Cooperative Cyber Defense Centre of Excellence in Tallinn.
- **Identify requirements for translators and interpreters early in the program.** This may be needed for specific requirements, such as an "ITAR-cleared" interpreter. Alternatively, consider adding permanent linguistic expertise to the Foreign Disclosure Office.

The relevant stakeholders are concept formulation and development, foreign disclosure, information security, manpower and training, and policy and SC planning.

Cross-Domain Barrier 3: Lack of Technical Collaborative Infrastructure Constrains the Ability of the United States and Its Allies and Partners to Share Information

The challenges raised by a lack of collaborative infrastructure have been observed in several air cases. Within the space domain, the WGS program had to overcome the lack of adequate platforms for information-sharing. In the cyber domain, a lack of collaborative infrastructure hindered collaboration generally and greatly slowed or limited information-sharing and the ability to respond to cyber incidents.

Sharing classified information can prove particularly difficult. Most U.S. partners do not have access to SIPRNet. The sharing of classified information (e.g., email, secure teleconferences) often takes place via BICES, which originally was designed for sharing intelligence in specific theaters of operation but subsequently expanded for broader information-sharing purposes. In some cases, the number of BICES machines is insufficient to ensure timely sharing of information. The lack of convenient, mutually acceptable systems for exchanging unclassified but sensitive information, as happened in the DTTI air-launched UAV case, is another type of technical barrier.

Potential mitigation strategies include the following:

- **Identify ways to improve the technical means for the communication and sharing of sensitive or classified information.**
- **Invest in collaborative infrastructure that uses artificial intelligence–enabled authentication and access** (zero-trust environments) rather than hardware workarounds (BICES terminals, SIPR REL, etc.). Zero-trust environments serve a similar function as the segregated environments enabled by hardware solutions but provide network and systems administrators with greater control to either authenticate or restrict access to sensitive information or specific segments of the network.

The relevant stakeholder communities are concept formulation and development and information security.

Cross-Domain Barrier 4: Slow Bureaucratic Execution Can Impede Security Cooperation

Despite support for collaboration at the senior-leader and tactical levels, we saw in several case studies (Wedgetail, ABMS, combined SC partnering, and F-35) bureaucratic and regulatory challenges impeding mid-level management's ability to make progress on implementation. This results in greater demands on the time of high-level U.S. officials and increases the risk that such demands might only be made for high-priority programs or allies and partners. In the space domain, we found a lack of middle-management capacity to be an issue, with too few personnel handling space cooperation at the Space and Missile Systems Center and within select Office of the Secretary of Defense organizations.

The Enhanced Polar System-Recapitalization case was a noteworthy exception, with proactive and highly involved mid-level officials, which resulted in a positive outcome. Similarly, the involvement of high-level officials was key to advancing the DTTI air-launched UAV case. This case exemplifies a good top-down approach in which high-level support helped enable the lower-level workers. In the Arctic MILSATCOM system case with Norway, DoD was able to mitigate the long timeline for MOA development by undertaking a parallel procurement process before finalizing the agreement. The flexibility of a parallel process for acquisition and MOA negotiations helped mitigate the challenges of the long legal and bureaucratic timeline.[89]

Potential mitigation strategies include the following:

- **Ensure the program has senior leadership attention** (i.e., has a "champion"). DAF leadership could initiate a review of all programs for which highly capable allies and partners are involved to ensure there is (1) a single-office point of contact and (2) a communication strategy in place for the more complex and more sensitive programs for which allies and partners do not have full access. Wedgetail and ABMS are examples of two cases that had no single champion and have been hampered by a lack of communication strategy.
- **Elevate issues quickly to senior leadership for arbitration**, especially if an issue has competing equities across bureaucracy.
- **Ensure the Foreign Disclosure Officer community has sufficient technical or domain-specific knowledge** (e.g., cyber subject-matter experts) and embed them within relevant organizations to make faster and more-confident foreign disclosure decisions.
- **Plan for the type and amount of expertise needed, as well as where this expertise will be found along the program's lifetime.** This might include the need for translators or interpreters. The risks of not having the right expertise should be documented and

---

89 Interview with U.S. government subject-matter expert, February 2021.

brought to the attention of senior leaders so that they can prioritize resources appropriately.

The relevant stakeholder communities are foreign disclosure, manpower and training, policy and SC planning, and weapons and acquisition.

Cross-Domain Barrier 5: Some U.S. Regulations Impede Rather Than Support Security Cooperation, Particularly with Fast-Evolving Technologies

Although there are established processes for U.S. systems that are sold to other countries, programs not of record and new initiatives—such as Wedgetail—require ad hoc processes. Each such program comes with its own idiosyncratic requirements for foreign disclosure and technology transfers that are demanding and complex. This is an issue, in particular, with technologies originating from allies. In the Wedgetail case, U.S. partners were reluctant to share the technologies they developed because they would lose control over them once they did.

More generally, rapidly evolving technology outpaces the development of (or updates to) U.S. regulations. As a result, some SC activities find themselves with new legal questions or confronting the need to set up ad hoc processes. It can be difficult to know how to apply the law to more-complicated and more-unusual SC activities. There may be a need to locate and then reach out to the right stakeholders (e.g., in major commands) rather than having a set process and to take a fresh look at technologies and assess whether processes are still applicable or whether they should be modified. For instance, the foreign disclosure process was not created with cyber data in mind. In some cases, bureaucratic processes prevent any information from being shared, much less shared quickly. Foreign disclosure processes lengthened the timelines in the WGS case.

Co-development projects present a variety of issues and information-sharing needs for the United States and its partners. In some cases, the United States needs to share a large amount of technical details and develop a capability to do so from the start. In other cases, the United States may share a finished product, co-develop an integration component, or expand an existing technology without sharing the underlying technical detail.

Finally, the rigidity of PAs prevents cooperation at the "speed of cyber" because the technology or threat might change. This was evident in both the U.S.-Australia and U.S.-Estonia cyber cooperation cases. Although this issue is most salient with new technologies, it can arise in other situations when U.S. bureaucratic and legal timelines make cooperation difficult to establish. This appeared in the Arctic MILSATCOM MOA and WGS cases.

Potential mitigation strategies include the following:

- **Develop cyber-specific disclosure policy and corresponding cyber security classification guidance.** The National Disclosure Committee could reconsider levels of risk acceptance and adapt the disclosure policy to current cyber needs. In the meantime, and until the new guidance is released, it would be useful to train additional foreign disclosure personnel who also have cyber subject matter expertise and place them in relevant directorates in U.S. Cyber Command and Combatant Commands to more rapidly and more confidently disclose technical information.

- **Develop adaptive cooperative agreement schemes** that enable quick changes in information sharing and SC activities in response to emerging crises (such as cyberattacks on sovereign or shared critical infrastructure). This contrasts with pursuing cyber cooperation primarily through the RDT&E MOU. In the Wedgetail case, the pursuit of novel avenues of U.S.-Australian-British collaboration on advancing radar technology helped keep things going when the program was otherwise engaged with executing the traditional foreign disclosure and licensing processes.
- **Review regulations** to ensure that they support the most efficient transfer of releasable technology between the United States and its allies or partners.
- **Ensure that experienced, well-trained staff can recognize when there are multiple ways to satisfy legal requirements** and generate flexible (ad hoc) processes that might help.
- **Engage foreign disclosure and information security communities early on to identify any known barriers to collaboration.**

The relevant stakeholder communities are foreign disclosure, manpower and training, and policy and SC planning.

Cross-Domain Barrier 6: Failing to Account for Ally's or Partner's Political Constraints Can Slow Cooperation Activities

In several cases, we found some political, organizational, or budgetary characteristics of the ally or partner that should have been well known (or at least somewhat anticipated) but were not. As a result, SC activities were slowed or impeded in multiple ways. For instance, the F-35 case showed the need for a flexible response to the ally's political constraints. The Arctic MILSATCOM case study—particularly, the MOA process—showed that cooperation with partners that have smaller space portfolios requires flexibility with funding mechanisms. In the cyber domain, cooperation with high-priority partners whose portfolio spans multiple civilian and military agencies (e.g., Estonia's "whole-of-society approach") requires flexibility when partnering with different U.S. agencies, which can be challenging if non-DoD agencies lack the required manpower or resources more generally.

Potential mitigation strategies include the following:

- **Ensure situational awareness among U.S. stakeholders of ally's or partner's internal constraints.** This could include systematically requiring a risk assessment at various points during the lifetime of a SC program.
- **Maintain a knowledge base of partner constraints.** This could be done through personnel incentives to remain engaged in SC efforts and retain the knowledge and understanding of partner processes. In cases in which personnel rotate, this practice could be done by ensuring that there is a proper handover of information and institutionalized

ways to maintain and update information regularly. Additionally, SAF/IA could add a section to the International Engagement Plan and the country blueprints that encourages SC planners—with input from others—to look for and capture partner internal constraints (e.g., in funding, manpower, politics, or bureaucratic practices). Such information should be made accessible to relevant stakeholders.

The relevant stakeholder communities are manpower and training and policy and SC planning.

Cross-Domain Barrier 7: Lack of Incentive, Tasking, and Understanding of Priorities for Combined Partnering in Third Countries

This barrier is particularly relevant for the air and cyber domains. In the cyber domain, the United States often gets inquiries from Eastern Partnership countries for support with cyber hygiene, cybersecurity, or how to implement e-governance initiatives. The United States cannot respond positively to these solicitations because of funding issues, a lack of agility, and a lack of prioritization of such combined partnering for countries that are willing to undertake the planned SC activities on their own.

Potential mitigation strategies include the following:

- **Review the first principles of SC with allies** to open the dialogue and expand opportunities for combined partnering in third countries where it makes the most sense from a strategic and implementation perspective.
- **Consider including combined SC partnering as a formal component of SC plans.** SAF/IA and A5 could be working with the air component commands to incorporate new thinking into existing SC planning documents regarding combined partnering, highlighting past successes and future opportunities. Oceania, a region that is of growing interest to the United States and that has allies with relevant experience, presence, and expertise, could be a good place to start.
- **Explore options for DoD to support allies' initiatives where appropriate in a planning process**, especially in countries where allies already have the bulk of experience and relationships. This could more effectively leverage the comparative advantages of allies.
- **Consult with allies to explore opportunities to partner on cyber and technical capacity-building in third countries.** It is possible, for example, to support another ally's efforts (such as Estonia) in a third country.

The relevant stakeholder communities are foreign disclosure and policy and SC planning.

Conclusion

Table 4.1 summarizes the above barriers, mitigation strategies, and stakeholder communities. Overall, we found that most of the barriers we identified exist across domains. Given our limited number of cases, we cannot determine whether domain-specific barriers also cross domains. Additional air and cyber cases might, for example, show a barrier that we only identified in the space domain. Regardless, the fact that at least some barriers can be found not only in different domains but also across different SC activities shows how prevalent they are. Addressing even a few of them could have a far-reaching impact on the success of SC activities across the DAF.

Table 4.2 summarizes the mitigation strategies we identified and the case studies to which they may apply. This table provides the reader with information on where to review for further information and some insights on the way strategies may cross domains and on similarities with some single-domain strategies. Again, we note that the single-domain strategies we identified may be applicable across domains but not in ways we were able to confirm, given our limited number of case studies.

Table 4.1. Barriers Identified and Relevant Stakeholder Communities

Barrier		Stakeholder Communities						
		Concept Formulation and Development	Foreign Disclosure	Information Security	Manpower and Training	Operations	Policy and SC Planning	Weapons and Acquisition
Domain-specific	Air: Differences in strategic priorities	X				X	X	
	Space: Complexity of space cooperation				X	X	X	X
	Space: Lack of human resources				X		X	
	Cyber: Understanding of "sensitive" data			X			X	
	Cyber: Prioritization issue		X				X	
Cross-domain	1. Involvement in concept development	X	X			X	X	
	2. Speed of communication	X	X	X	X		X	
	3. Lack of technical infrastructure	X	X	X	X		X	
	4. Slow bureaucratic execution		X		X		X	X
	5. Regulations and new technologies		X		X		X	
	6. Ally's or partner's political constraints				X		X	X
	7. Combined partnering		X				X	

Table 4.2. Mitigation Strategies to Cross-Domain Barriers, with Related Case Studies

Strategy	Related Case Studies
• Review guidance and policies regarding the incorporation of allies in early concept development and acquisition • Consider alternative ways to involve allies and partners in key concept development discussions and programs beyond nonreciprocal exchanges • Reexamine the potential impact of not sharing advances in technology with closest allies	• ABMS • F-35 Co-Production • QZSS • U.S.-Australia
• Provide incentive in policy, guidance, and senior-leader statements to encourage the release of information and technology to specific groups or countries • Incentivize sharing while disincentivizing defaulting to NOFORN • Streamline communications by ensuring allies and partners are fully aware of the government-to-government channels throughout the process • During early discussions on a program, agree with the ally or partner on standard operating procedures for the communication of sensitive but unclassified information	• ABMS • E-7 Wedgetail • WGS • Arctic MILSATCOM System • QZSS • U.S.-Australia • U.S.-Estonia
• Leverage personnel exchanges and foreign exchange officers within the RDT&E community, as well as within the operational, acquisition, and domain-specific commands • Place designated, domain-specific LNOs at equivalent organizations in ally and partner countries and at relevant Centers of Excellence	• ABMS • E-7 Wedgetail • WGS • QZSS • U.S.-Australia • U.S.-Estonia
• Identify requirements for translators and interpreters early in the program	• QZSS • U.S.-Estonia
• Identify ways to improve the technical means for communication and the sharing of sensitive or classified information	• WGS • Arctic MILSATCOM System • QZSS • U.S.-Australia • U.S.-Estonia • U.S.-Finland
• Invest in collaborative infrastructure that uses artificial intelligence–enabled authentication and access	• WGS • U.S.-Australia • U.S.-Estonia • U.S.-Finland
• Ensure the program has senior leadership attention	• ABMS • E-7 Wedgetail • F-35 Co-Production • Air-Launched UAV • Combined SC Partnering • WGS • Arctic MILSATCOM System • QZSS

Strategy	Related Case Studies
• Elevate issues quickly to senior leadership for arbitration	• ABMS • E-7 Wedgetail • F-35 Co-Production • WGS • Arctic MILSATCOM System • QZSS
• Ensure the Foreign Disclosure Officer community has sufficient technical or domain-specific knowledge	• ABMS • E-7 Wedgetail • F-35 Co-Production • WGS • Arctic MILSATCOM System • QZSS
• Plan for the type and amount of expertise needed, as well as where this expertise will be found along the programs' lifetime	• ABMS • E-7 Wedgetail • F-35 Co-Production • QZSS
• Develop adaptive cooperative agreement schemes	• E-7 Wedgetail • F-35 Co-Production • QZSS • U.S.-Australia • U.S.-Estonia
• Engage foreign disclosure and information security communities early on to identify any barriers to collaboration	• E-7 Wedgetail • F-35 Co-Production • WGS • Arctic MILSATCOM System • QZSS • U.S.-Australia • U.S.-Estonia
• Ensure that experienced, well-trained staff can recognize when there are multiple ways to satisfy legal requirements	• E-7 Wedgetail • F-35 Co-Production • WGS • Arctic MILSATCOM System • U.S.-Australia • U.S.-Estonia
• Review regulations	• E-7 Wedgetail • F-35 Co-Production • U.S.-Australia • U.S.-Estonia
• Ensure situational awareness among U.S. stakeholders of an ally's or partner's internal constraints	• F-35 Co-Production • Combined SC Partnering • Air-Launched UAV • WGS • Arctic MILSATCOM System • QZSS • U.S.-Estonia • U.S.-Finland
• Maintain a knowledge base of partner constraints	• F-35 Co-Production • Combined SC Partnering • Air-Launched UAV • Arctic MILSATCOM System • U.S.-Estonia • U.S.-Finland

Strategy	Related Case Studies
• Review the first principles of SC with allies • Consider including combined SC partnering as a formal component of SC plans	• Combined SC Partnering
• Explore options for DoD to support allies' initiatives where appropriate in a planning process	• Wedgetail • Combined SC Partnering • U. S.-Australia • U.S.-Estonia • U.S.-Finland
• Consult with allies to explore opportunities to partner on cyber and technical capacity-building in third countries • Develop cyber-specific disclosure policy and corresponding cybersecurity classification guidance	• Combined SC Partnering • U.S.-Australia • U.S.-Estonia • U.S.-Finland

We found that adapting SC processes is a challenge across air, space, and cyber domains. This is especially true when fast-evolving technologies (e.g., Wedgetail) are involved, SC activities rely on new collaboration constructs (i.e., those, such as the Arctic MILSATCOM program, for which the United States does not have a program of reference) or complex ones (e.g., for the ABMS); and when there is a rapidly changing and constantly evolving environment and threats, as in the cyber domain.

Other observations point to the need for deep dives on subsets of allies/partners or SC program types. In our case studies, the risk level of removing some barriers depends on the ally/partner or program; whether the United States or its ally/partner was the main "culprit" for the barriers varied across cases. More fundamentally, we did not explore the operational risks—the potential effect on coalition warfighting—of barriers that hamper integration with allies, a critical issue about which there is little understanding. Any attempt at defining broad patterns of risk or responsibility would require a larger body of research.

Chapter 5. Conclusion

Overall, we find that many barriers are interconnected, adding complexity to both the problem and the solution. Our domain-specific and cross-domain mitigation strategies (about 35 in total) focus on limitations in strategy and policy, planning and approach, and manpower and training. Some are targeted at SAF/IA and A5, some at DAF leadership, and others at higher levels within DoD or even more broadly with the State Department or Congress. Some highlight laws that would need to be adjusted (such as ITAR restrictions on technology that originates in foreign countries and that the United States acquires). All have been offered for the DAF's consideration and are intended to stimulate discussion. With only 11 case studies, emphasizing depth over breadth, we have to be cautious about drawing broad conclusions and making specific recommendations. Still, our research pointed to a few key areas in which action could allow the DAF to make significant advances in the short term to address some of the pervasive barriers noted in this report.

In trying to determine the rough level of effort required to implement a specific mitigation strategy, it may be useful to consider the following questions: Does the action need to be taken by the United States or its ally or partner? By the DAF or another U.S. government agency? By one community (e.g., concept formulation and development, foreign disclosure, information security, manpower and training, operations, SC policy and planning, or weapons and acquisition)? Or by multiple communities, perhaps with no one clear leader? We expect that the more stakeholders that are involved (particularly, those outside SAF/IA/A5 and the DAF), the harder it will be to change processes and habits, making overcoming a given barrier more difficult and requiring time, commitment, patience, and (possibly) money. However, we do not make assumptions regarding how the number and type of the stakeholders involved might affect the implementation of mitigation strategies, since this would depend on the specifics of each SC case. In some instances, it might be easier to influence an ally's or partner's ways than to change one's own (we found that the DAF operates largely in silos as far as allies and partners are concerned), whereas the opposite is true in other cases.

Four Priority Strategies to Consider

In this section, we provide some initial insights into how the DAF might respond to the domain-specific and the cross-domain barriers, as well as how it might implement some mitigation strategies, particularly those that require limited resources and lower risk. We focus here on four key priority strategies, in no particular order, that present the highest potential payoff for SAF/IA and, by extension, the DAF. The strategies were selected according to the following factors:

- They can be implemented by the United States and are not dependent on actions undertaken by allies and partners.
- They can be implemented largely by SAF/IA, or SAF/IA and a limited number of other DAF or DoD organizations that SAF/IA works closely with.
- They cover a large number of the approximately 35 mitigation strategies suggested by our case studies, either within a single domain or across domains.

The following points focus mainly on manpower and expertise, streamlining communication with allies and partners, and improving information-sharing platforms.

First, **the DAF and allies and partners would benefit from a review of the legal authorities for the roles and the placement of exchanges, nonreciprocal exchanges, and LNOs, many of which are legacy positions**. Information-sharing challenges were a recurrent theme throughout our case studies. Increasing bilateral defense exchanges in RDT&E and in cooperative development to improve coordination and understanding of expectations, capabilities, and needs could help address these challenges, but there are legal issues pertaining to what sensitive information exchange officers can share with their home country and the levels of classification that LNOs can typically have access to. Although this strategy would require some policy changes (and, potentially, changes to U.S. law), it might be worth exploring a new hybrid status between exchange officer and LNO positions that would allow for more information-sharing with highly capable allies and partners within set limits.

Second, **given the increase in demand for technical expertise in new and growing SC domains (space, cyber), it would be helpful to ensure that the foreign disclosure community is enabled with sufficient technical or domain-specific expertise** (and embedded in the relevant organizations) to make rapid decisions. Because of the services' funding constraints for new manpower requirements, it will be critical to engage the Defense Security Cooperation Agency on this issue to approve funding for additional expertise in cyber and space to support foreign disclosure positions. Space- and cyber-specific disclosure policy and corresponding security classification guidance would increase the benefit realized from the proposed infusion of needed disclosure expertise and capacity.

Third, **it would be useful to look for ways for the DAF to improve its advocacy for the inclusion of international equities throughout a program's life cycle**. It is important for DAF leadership to understand, for example, why it is often quite difficult to include highly capable allies and partners in the early stages of concept development. Some acknowledgment of the current disconnects, framed around our case studies, could be the first step toward problem-solving and crafting a more integrated approach to working with allies and partners. This could include the identification of a DAF "champion" for each major U.S. capability development initiative to improve transparency and accountability internally and streamline communications with highly capable allies and partners. Ensuring timely senior leader (within and outside the DAF) attention on issues for which there is internal U.S. government disagreement (e.g., security-related risk tolerance) could help reduce the friction from the complex, distributed U.S.

system. In more concrete terms, DAF leadership could initiate a review of major acquisition programs in which highly capable allies and partners are involved to ensure there is (1) a single-office point of contact and a single coordinating authority to lead negotiations and (2) a communication strategy in place for the more complex and more sensitive programs for which allies and partners do not have full access. Further efforts to reduce U.S. complexity, which can be daunting for allies and partners, could include centralizing functions, where practical (e.g., creating a joint terminal program for operations or a single point of contact for partners for space SC). DAF leadership could engage the Office of the Under Secretary of Defense for Policy, the Office of the Under Secretary of Defense for Acquisition and Sustainment, and other senior DoD communities to ensure that policy is up-to-date and matches the strategic intent of DoD leadership. Coordinating bodies, such as the International Space Cooperation Enterprise Working Group, could be empowered to provide specific recommendations that apply across the DAF and beyond. Finally, DAF guidance to reduce the impacts of these barriers could be developed and stated as a priority in the DAF International Engagement Plan.

Fourth, **the DAF would benefit from supporting additional allied and partner access to collaborative platforms to facilitate cooperation and information-sharing**. Cyber cooperation, in particular, could benefit from such efforts. This could include developing secure collaborative infrastructure between the United States and partner cyber organizations to discuss issues that may be unclassified for the United States but classified for partners (or the other way around). More broadly, this could increase the information security community's role in working with allies and partners to (1) develop a shared understanding of what is sensitive and (2) establish security controls that protect the information in a way that meets cyber community operational needs and addresses U.S. intelligence and technology protection concerns. In the cyber domain, ways to overcome recurrent information-sharing issues might include investing in collaborative infrastructure that uses artificial intelligence–enabled authentication and access (zero-trust environments) rather than hardware workarounds (BICES terminals, SIPR REL, etc.).

Good Practices for Consideration: Culture, Approach, and Attitude

Throughout this study, our team had the rare opportunity to speak with both U.S. and allied and partner officials about specific challenges related to working together. Some of the broader, more strategic insights do not tie neatly to a single case study but instead reflect broader, pervasive issues that could be mitigated by changing mindsets and, perhaps, by altering some practices. The ideas we list here, developed from the interviews we conducted for our case studies, are good practices for policymakers and practitioners to consider.[90]

Encourage the SC planning community to gain a better understanding of how key allies and partners are structured to support engagement with the United States and what

---

[90] See Moroney and Tidwell, 2021.

limitations they have (e.g., policies, priorities, personnel). Examples of the most common barriers, perhaps those identified in this report, could be integrated into the *International Engagement Plan* and other country-level planning documents, such as the country blueprints.

Engage with allies about their regional and country priorities, their international engagement approaches with third countries, and how they might wish to work with the United States in partner countries that are of high interest to both.

Seek information from allies and partners about collaboration barriers and precisely how they are affected by these barriers; share these insights across communities. The barrier typology can serve as a guide for the DAF to systematically track inefficiencies, as well as the initiatives and programs in which such inefficiencies recur. This will form an evidence base to develop more-specific mitigation strategies.

Address barriers head-on in bilateral and multilateral contexts, planning events, standing forums, and other domain-specific communities, wherever possible; look to allies and partners for ideas on solutions, and follow up. Barriers to working together could be a formal component of all Air Senior National Representative talks, Operator Engagement Talks, and other bilateral SC activities to try to identify issues early and head them off. HAF A5 could connect to HAF A3 and component commands to ensure that barriers are included in wargames. SAF/IA could leverage its positive relationship with the Office of the Under Secretary of Defense for Acquisition and Sustainment to problem-solve. Issues that cannot be addressed at this level could be raised at a higher level.

Ensure that relevant DAF communities (beyond SC planners) are represented in allied and partner bilateral meetings and other key senior leader–led events. Subject-matter experts from the Foreign Disclosure Office, information security, concept development, and acquisition could be invited to take part, review plans, and comment.

Potential Future Directions: We See Many Analysis Avenues

This research is intended to start a more focused conversation regarding barriers that affect highly capable allies and partners. We recognize the challenge of providing a set of specific recommendations, given the evidence that we have from 11 case studies. To pinpoint some possible next steps, we identified the following questions that could be developed into additional analytic efforts, some of which may be suitable for the DAF to do internally while others would likely require a more complex effort involving other U.S. actors or changes involving U.S. allies and partners:

- What are the strategic and operational implications of key barriers with highly capable allies and partners? What is the operational risk of not sharing the information that allies and partners need?
- What types of barriers exist in collaborating with countries with less capability or those that are less closely aligned with the United States? How do these barriers differ from those found in collaboration with highly capable allies?

- How can DoD build more flexibility into its collaborative agreements to enable the United States and partner nations to respond to unforeseen crises, cyber incidents or attacks, or emerging threats?
- What options exist for accelerating foreign disclosure processes, and what would be the associated risks?
- In what aspects of partnering efforts should the United States be taking more risks? What and who is involved in understanding and accepting greater risk, where necessary?

One of the final points to make with this study, which we heard time and again from allied and partner officials, is how important it is to take the time to listen and seek clarification to better understand their strategies and perspectives, take their concerns into consideration, and actively problem-solve together. In the past, the United States set the pace for capability development. There are at least a few recent examples (QZSS, Arctic MILSATCOM MOA, and Wedgetail) that demonstrate that this may not always be the case in the future. Allies and partners do not want to be left behind from a capabilities and acquisition perspective. It can be challenging for allies to make internal defense investment decisions if they do not have a clear picture of where DoD is going. If their concerns are regularly overlooked and if DoD overclassifies critical information regularly and does not clarify its position on sharing information, opportunities to collaborate will be jeopardized. In terms of SC, although DoD and the DAF have many times the resources that key allies do, these organizations do not have to execute unilaterally or lead in every instance. Sometimes it is more effective to plan out activities that build on successful efforts already being carried out by a key ally in a third country, such as the efforts of Australia, France, and New Zealand in Oceania. Overall, it is important to recognize the distinct capabilities, experience, and expertise of allies and partners and to actively look for ways to reduce or eliminate barriers to collaboration.

In this report, we link the mitigation strategies with the relevant stakeholder communities that the DAF would work with to problem-solve together. We suggest the DAF focus mostly on the options intended to improve SC planning and that senior DAF leadership focus on improving coordination and communication among the various stakeholder communities. We recognize that some of the mitigation strategies are easier to implement than others and that the more difficult strategies are worthy of further study and analysis to determine the most appropriate way ahead.

Abbreviations

ABMS	Advanced Battle Management System
BICES	Battlefield Information Collection and Exploitation System
COVID-19	coronavirus disease 2019
DAF	Department of the Air Force
DoD	U.S. Department of Defense
DTTI	Defense Technology and Trade Initiative
FVEY	Five Eyes
HAF	Headquarters, Department of the Air Force
ITAR	International Traffic in Arms Regulations
JADC2	Joint All-Domain Command and Control
LNO	liaison officer
MILSATCOM	military satellite communications
MOA	Memorandum of Agreement
MOU	Memorandum of Understanding
NATO	North Atlantic Treaty Organization
NOFORN	Not Releasable to Foreign Nationals
PA	project agreement
QZSS	Quazi-Zenith Satellite System
RDT&E	research, development, testing, and evaluation
SAF/IA	Secretary of the Air Force for International Affairs
SATCOM	satellite communications
SC	security cooperation
SIGINT	signals intelligence
SIPR REL	SIPRNet Releasable
UAV	unmanned aerial vehicle
UK	United Kingdom
WGS	Wideband Global Satellite Communications

References

Australian National Audit Office, *'Wedgetail' Airborne Early Warning and Control Aircraft: Project Management*, Canberra, Australia, 2004.

———, *2014–2015 Major Projects Report*, Canberra, Australia, 2016.

"Australia's Troubled E-7A 'Wedgetail' AWACS Program," *Defense Industry Daily*, May 3, 2021.

Binnendijk, Anika, Gene Germanovich, Bruce McClintock, and Sarah Heintz, *At the Vanguard: European Contributions to NATO's Future Combat Airpower*, Santa Monica, Calif.: RAND Corporation, RR-A311-1, 2020. As of April 12, 2022:
https://www.rand.org/pubs/research_reports/RRA311-1.html

Borys, Stephanie, "Licence to Hack: Using a Keyboard to Fight Islamic State," *ABC News Australia*, December 17, 2019.

Burgess, Stephen F., "Military Intervention in Africa: French and US Approaches Compared," *Journal of European, Middle Eastern, and African Affairs*, Vol. 1, No. 1, Spring 2019, pp. 69–89.

Canadian Department of National Defence, Danish Ministry of Defence, Luxembourgish Minister of Defence, Dutch Minister of Defence, New Zealand Defence Force, and U.S. Department of Defence, Memorandum of Understanding Among the Department of National Defence of Canada and the Ministry of Defence of the Kingdom of Denmark and the Minister of Defence of the Grand Duchy of Luxembourg and the Minister of Defence of the Kingdom of the Netherlands and the New Zealand Defence Force and the Department of Defense of the United States of America Concerning the Joint Production, Operations, and Support of Wideband Global Satellite Communications, 2012, as amended in 2017 with the addition of the Danish Ministry of Defence.

Carey, Bill "Italy Begins F-35 Assembly; Dutch Store Their First Two Jets" AINonline, July 26, 2013.

Chaney, Andrus W., "Implementing Guidance for Security Cooperation: Overcoming Obstacles to U.S. Africa Command's Efforts," *Joint Force Quarterly*, No. 88, 1st Quarter 2018, pp. 91–100.

Cordey, Sean, "Finland," in Robert S. Dewar, ed., *National Cybersecurity and Cyberdefense Policy Snapshots*, Zürich, Switzerland: Center for Security Studies, September 2018, pp. 24–42.

Danish Ministry of Defence, *NORDEFCO Annual Report 2020*, Copenhagen, 2020.

Department of Defense Instruction 5000.80, *Operation of the Middle Tier of Acquisition (MTA)*, Washington, D.C.: U.S. Department of Defense, December 30, 2019.

DoD—*See* U.S. Department of Defense.

Garamone, Jim, "U.S. Begins Process of 'Unwinding' Turkey from F-35 Program, DoD Officials Say," U.S. Department of Defense, July 17, 2019. As of November 9, 2020: https://www.defense.gov/Explore/News/Article/Article/1908351/us-begins-process-of-unwinding-turkey-from-f-35-program-dod-officials-say/

"Germany, Italy Protest at U.S. Axing of Missile Defense Funding," Reuters, February 2, 2013.

Goldfein, Peter, and André Adamson, "The Trilateral Strategic Initiative: A Primer for Developing Future Airpower Cooperation," *Air & Space Power Journal*, Vol. 30, No. 4, Winter 2016, pp. 74–82.

Hitchens, Theresa, "Air Force Eyes European ABMS Demo in Spring," *Breaking Defense*, June 29, 2020.

Hoehn, John R., "Joint All-Domain Command and Control: Background and Issues for Congress," Washington, D.C.: Congressional Research Service, R46725, March 18, 2021.

Hoff, Rachel, "Next Steps for U.S.-Japan Security Cooperation," Sasakawa USA, June 8, 2016.

Insinna, Valerie, "Top U.S. Air Force General Isn't Ready to Buy E-7 Wedgetail Just Yet," *Defense News*, February 26, 2021.

Inspector General of the U.S. Department of Defense, *DoD Evaluation of Over-Classification of National Security Information*, Alexandria, Va., September 30, 2013.

———, *Follow Up to DoD Evaluation of Over-Classification of National Security Information*, Alexandria, Va., December 1, 2016.

Joint Chiefs of Staff, *The National Military Strategy of the United States of America*, Washington, D.C., June 2015.

Joint Publication 3-20, *Security Cooperation*, Washington, D.C.: Joint Chiefs of Staff, May 23, 2017.

Kelly, Terrence, Jefferson P. Marquis, Cathryn Quantic Thurston, Jennifer D. P. Moroney, and Charlotte Lynch, *Security Cooperation Organizations in the Country Team: Options for Success*, Santa Monica, Calif.: RAND Corporation, TR-734-A, 2010. As of April 14, 2022: https://www.rand.org/pubs/technical_reports/TR734.html

Kenlon, Frank, "IA&E in the Adaptive Acquisition Framework (AAF)," Defense Acquisition University, November 12, 2020.

Kim, Yool, Elliot Axelband, Abby Doll, Mel Eisman, Myron Hura, Edward G. Keating, Martin C. Libicki, Bradley Martin, Michael E. McMahon, Jerry M. Sollinger, Erin York, Mark V. Arena, Irv Blickstein, and William Shelton, *Acquisition of Space Systems, Volume 7: Past Problems and Future Challenges*, Santa Monica, Calif.: RAND Corporation, MG-1171/7-OSD, 2015. As of May 14, 2021:
https://www.rand.org/pubs/monographs/MG1171z7.html

Laird, Robbin, "Lessons Learned at Cameri, Italy's F-35 HQ: Implications for Asia," *Breaking Defense*, November 4, 2013.

Mayer, Daryl, "India, US Sign Air-Launched UAV Co-Development Project Agreement," U.S. Air Force, September 3, 2021. As of September 30, 2021:
https://www.af.mil/News/Article-Display/Article/2764056/india-us-sign-air-launched-uav-co-development-project-agreement/

Mehta, Aaron, "US, India Collaborating on Air-Launched Drone," *Defense News*, March 18, 2019. As of September 30, 2021:
https://www.defensenews.com/global/asia-pacific/2019/03/18/us-india-collaborating-on-air-launched-drone/

Moroney, Jennifer D. P., Stephanie Pezard, David E. Thaler, Gene Germanovich, Beth Grill, Bruce McClintock, Karen Schwindt, Mary Kate Adgie, Anika Binnendijk, Kevin J. Connolly, Katie Feistel, Jeffrey W. Hornung, Alison K. Hottes, Moon Kim, Isabelle Nazha, Gabrielle Tarini, Mark Toukan, and Jalen Zeman, *Overcoming Barriers to Working with Highly Capable Allies and Partners in the Air, Space, and Cyber Domains: Case Studies*, Santa Monica, Calif.: RAND Corporation, RR-A968-2, 2023, Not available to the general public.

Moroney, Jennifer D. P., and Alan Tidwell, "America's Strategy in Oceania: Time for a Better Approach," *War on the Rocks*, July 19, 2021.

Moroney, Jennifer D. P., Celeste Ward Gventer, Stephanie Pezard, and Laurence Smallman, *Lessons from U.S. Allies in Security Cooperation with Third Countries: The Cases of Australia, France, and the United Kingdom*, Santa Monica, Calif.: RAND Corporation, TR-972-AF, 2011. As of April 15, 2022:
https://www.rand.org/pubs/technical_reports/TR972.html

Obecny, Kristina, and Gregory Sanders, *U.S.-Canadian Defense Industrial Cooperation*, Washington, D.C.: Center for Strategic and International Studies, June 2017.

Pancevski, Bojan, and Sara Germano, "Drop Huawei or See Intelligence Sharing Pared Back, U.S. Tells Germany," *Wall Street Journal*, March 11, 2019.

Pernin, Christopher G., Jakub P. Hlavka, Matthew E. Boyer, John Gordon IV, Michael Lerario, Jan Osburg, Michael Shurkin, and Daniel C. Gibson, *Targeted Interoperability: A New*

Imperative for Multinational Operations, Santa Monica, Calif.: RAND Corporation, RR-2075-A, 2019. As of April 15, 2022:
https://www.rand.org/pubs/research_reports/RR2075.html

Pomerleau, Mark, "How Cyber Command Can Limit the Reach of ISIS," *C4ISRNET*, September 17, 2019.

Ramani, Samuel, "France and the United States Are Making West Africa's Security Situation Worse," *Foreign Policy*, September 12, 2020.

Riposo, Jessie, Megan McKernan, Jeffrey A. Drezner, Geoffrey McGovern, Daniel Tremblay, Jason Kumar, and Jerry M. Sollinger, *Issues with Access to Acquisition Data and Information in the Department of Defense: Executive Summary*, Santa Monica, Calif.: RAND Corporation, RR-880/1-OSD, 2015. As of April 15, 2022:
https://www.rand.org/pubs/research_reports/RR880z1.html

Ross, Thomas W., "Enhancing Security Cooperation Effectiveness: A Model for Capability Package Planning," *Joint Force Quarterly*, No. 80, January 2016, pp. 25–34.

SAF/IA—*See* Secretary of the Air Force for International Affairs.

Secretary of the Air Force for International Affairs, *Department of the Air Force International Engagement Plan*, Washington, D.C., July 2020.

Sirota, Sara, "Air Force Confronting Defense Cooperation Challenges with Allies During COVID-19," *Inside Defense*, April 28, 2020.

Skorupski, Bolko J., and Nina M. Serafino, *DOD Security Cooperation: An Overview of Authorities and Issues*, Washington, D.C.: Congressional Research Service, R44602, August 23, 2016.

Tatsumi, Yuki, "Introduction" in Yuki Tatsumi, ed., *US-Japan-Australia Security Cooperation: Prospects and Challenges*, Washington, D.C.: Stimson Center, April 2015a, pp. 15–22.

———, "US-Japan-Australia Cooperation in Defense Equipment: Untapped Potential or a Bridge Too Far?" in Yuki Tatsumi, ed., *US-Japan-Australia Security Cooperation: Prospects and Challenges*, Washington, D.C.: Stimson Center, April 2015b, pp. 77–90.

Taylor, Rob, "U.S., New Zealand End Rift over Nuclear-Weapons Policies," *Wall Street Journal*, July 21, 2016.

U.S. Air Force, "Wideband Global SATCOM Satellite," webpage, November 23, 2015. As of January 29, 2019:
https://www.af.mil/About-Us/Fact-Sheets/Display/Article/104512/wideband-global-satcom-satellite

———, "India and US Sign Project Agreement for Air-Launched Unmanned Aerial Vehicle," press release, Arlington, Va., September 3, 2021. As of September 30, 2021: https://www.af.mil/News/Article-Display/Article/2764069/india-and-us-sign-project-agreement-for-air-launched-unmanned-aerial-vehicle/

U.S. Air Force and Norwegian Ministry of Defence, Arctic Satellite Communications Memorandum of Agreement, May 28, 2019.

U.S. Cyber Command, "US and Australia Sign First-Ever Cyber Agreement To Develop Virtual Training Range," press release, Fort George G. Meade, Md., December 4, 2020.

U.S. Department of Defense, *Sustaining U.S. Global Leadership: Priorities for 21st Century Defense*, Washington, D.C., January 2012.

———, "U.S., Estonia Sign Defense Research Agreement," June 22, 2016.

———, *Summary: Department of Defense Cyber Strategy 2018*, Washington, D.C., 2018a.

———, *Summary of the 2018 National Defense Strategy of the United States: Sharpening the American Military's Competitive Edge*, Washington, D.C., 2018b.

———, *Selected Acquisition Report: Wideband Global SATCOM (WGS) as of FY2020 President's Budget*, Washington, D.C., December 2018c.

———, *Defense Space Strategy Summary*, Washington, D.C., June 2020.

———, "Fact Sheet: 2022 National Defense Strategy," March 28, 2022.

U.S. Department of Defense and Australian Department of Defence, Memorandum of Understanding Between the Department of Defense of the United States of America and the Department of Defence of Australia Concerning Joint Production, Operations, and Support of Wideband Global Satellite Communications, Washington, D.C., November 14, 2007.

U.S. Department of Defense and Finnish Ministry of Defense, Statement of Intent Between the Department of Defense of the United States and the Ministry of Defense of the Republic of Finland, Helsinki, October 7, 2016.

U.S. Department of State, "Joint Statement on the Sixth Meeting of the U.S.-Japan Comprehensive Dialogue on Space," July 24, 2019.

U.S. Department of State, Office of the Spokesperson, "Joint Statement on the Sixth Meeting of the U.S.-Japan Comprehensive Dialogue on Space," July 24, 2019.

U.S. Government Accountability Office, "Conventional Arms Transfer Policy: Agency Processes for Reviewing Direct Commercial Sales and Foreign Military Sales Align with Policy Criteria," Washington, D.C., September 9, 2019. As of November 2, 2020: https://www.gao.gov/assets/710/701248.pdf

Wacker, Gudrun, *Security Cooperation in East Asia: Structures, Trends and Limitations*, Berlin: German Institute for International and Security Affairs, May 2015.

The White House, *Interim National Security Strategic Guidance*, Washington, D.C., March 2021.